THE ALDINE EDITION

OF THE BRITISH

POETS

THE POEMS OF HENRY HOWARD

EARL OF SURREY

H.Robinsou sc.

.RY H⋅⋅.ARD

⋅ SURREY

⋅ ⋅⋅⋅

⋅ ⋅ONS. YORK STREET

⋅ ⋅ GARDEN

H.Robinson sc.

THE

POEMS OF HENRY HOWARD

EARL OF SURREY

LONDON

GEORGE BELL & SONS, YORK STREET

COVENT GARDEN

CHISWICK PRESS :—C. WHITTINGHAM AND CO., TOOKS COURT, CHANCERY LANE.

ADVERTISEMENT.

THE present work, although substantially a reprint of the Aldine edition of "The Poetical Works of the Earl of Surrey," published in 1831, has been critically and carefully revised, and some additional notes appended explanatory of words now become obsolete. The Poems have been collated with the edition of the "Songs and Sonnets," edited by Bishop Percy and George Steevens, as well as by the recent reprint of the first edition of "Tottel's Miscellany," by John Payne Collier, Esq., whose ready kindness is acknowledged for the loan of the sheets of that rare work. The text of the two books of "Virgil's Æneid," has also been revised by the accurate edition of William Bolland, Esq. published by the Roxburghe Club.

In the Memoir of the Earl of Surrey, some of the statements of his heroic career have been corrected, and other particulars relating to him supplied, which had escaped the researches of Dr. Nott and his later biographers.

CONTENTS.

INDEX OF FIRST LINES.

MEMOIR OF HENRY HOWARD,

EARL OF SURREY.

" I write of him whose fame for aye endures."
Turbervile's Epitaph on Surrey.

ISTINGUISHED alike by his talents and rank, HENRY HOWARD EARL OF SURREY has attracted considerable attention; and as the first writer who attempted to refine our language, and to rescue English poetry from the grossness for which the productions of his predecessors are remarkable, he is worthy of the extraordinary research which his latest biographer has displayed in collecting particulars respecting his history. Dr. Nott affords a very creditable example of industry, and it is no slight praise to say that he appears to have exhausted every available source of information. The following Memoir has, therefore, been drawn up almost entirely from materials collected by Dr. Nott; an admission which it would be disingenuous to withhold: but considerable difference

will be found with respect to the inferences
which that writer has drawn from some of the
facts he has brought to light; and it is from this
circumstance that these sheets derive their claim
to attention. The most interesting of the letters
which occur in the appendix to Dr. Nott's edition are here introduced into the Memoir, and
though the present narrative is destitute of those
pleasing speculations which distinguish that
biographer's Life of Surrey, the loss may, perhaps, be borne with, when it is remembered
that it is as dangerous for a biographer as for an
historian to indulge his *imaginative* powers.

Although the Earl of Surrey owes but little of
the respect which is felt for his memory to the
adventitious splendour of his birth, it is necessary
to speak of his genealogy with some minuteness,
because it was from circumstances arising out
of his pedigree that he became one of the victims
of Henry the Eighth.

Doubts have been expressed as to the remote
antiquity of the family of Howard; but it is beyond dispute that they descend from Sir William
Howard, the Chief Justice of the Common Pleas
in the reigns of Edward the First and Second,
whose son, Sir John, was a Knight Banneret as
early as 1307. His great great grandson, Sir
Robert Howard, married Margaret Mowbray,
daughter of Thomas, Duke of Norfolk and Earl
Marshal, whose mother was Elizabeth, daughter
and heiress of John, Lord Segrave, the grand-
daughter and heiress of Thomas de Brotherton,
Earl of Norfolk, a younger son of King Edward

the First.   Sir John Howard, K.G., the eldest
son of Sir Robert by the Lady Margaret Mowbray, was created a Baron in 1470; and on the
extinction of the Mowbrays, Dukes of Norfolk,
about the year 1480, he became, in right of his
mother, the eldest coheir of that house, which
entitled him to quarter whatever arms were borne
by them, a fact, as will afterwards appear, of
some importance.   Sir John Howard was raised
to the dukedom of Norfolk by Richard the
Third, who at the same time created his eldest
son, Thomas, Earl of Surrey.   These titles were
forfeited after the battle of Bosworth, in which
the " Jocky of Norfolk" gallantly fell in the
cause of his sovereign and benefactor.

Thomas Howard, his son, was restored to the
earldom of Surrey in 1489; and in reward of
his services at Flodden Field he was created
Duke of Norfolk, in February, 1514.   Dying in
1524, he was succeeded by his son Thomas, third
Duke of Norfolk, who was twice married—first
to Anne, daughter of King Edward the Fourth,
by whom he had no issue that survived their
childhood, and secondly to Elizabeth Stafford,
eldest daughter of Edward, Duke of Buckingham, by whom he was father of the Poet.   His
second marriage, which proved an unhappy one,
took place soon after Easter in 1512; the Duchess
was twenty years younger than her husband,
and was then the object of an attachment, which
was reciprocal, to the Earl of Westmorland.

The exact date of the birth of the Earl of
Surrey has not been ascertained, but it may be

assigned to some time between 1516 and 1518;
nor has it been determined where it occurred,
though many circumstances render it probable
that it took place either at Framlingham or Tendring Hall, in Suffolk.[1]

It seems probable that Surrey was educated,
if not wholly, at least in part, by an eminent
scholar of the name of John Clerke, who having
passed some time on the Continent, where he
acquired a perfect acquaintance with the French
and the Italian languages, was afterwards received into the Duke of Norfolk's family, and
lived with him in the house as his secretary,
until the time of the Duke's attainder and imprisonment. Clerke's work, " De Mortuorum
Resurrectione, et Extremo Judicio," 4to, 1545,
is dedicated to Surrey,[2] and his " Treatise of
Nobility," 12mo, 1543, to his father, the Duke
of Norfolk. In the latter work Clerke mentions
with the highest commendations many transla-
tions done by Surrey, from the Latin, Italian,
French, and Spanish languages. But these, it
is probable, were nothing more than juvenile

[1] In an account of the fare of Henry Howard in the nursery at Tendring Hall, there appears to be for his breakfast
throughout the year, " a racke or chyne of mutton, and a
checkyn," except on Fridays and Saturdays, when it is " a
dysshe of butter-mylke and six eggs." (Catering Book of
Thomas, Earl of Surrey, third Duke of Norfolk, for 1523, a
MS. in the possession of Sir Thomas Phillipps.) This book
proves that Surrey was in his youth always at home with
the other children.

[2] A copy of this work in the British Museum has the
following manuscript note:—" The author of this tract was
preceptor to Henry Howard, Earl of Surrey, to whom it is
dedicated."

exercises. It appears that Clerke practised necromancy, which may account for Surrey's faith in judicial astrology.

Bred up in the country, Surrey acquired an early fondness for active pursuits. As he advanced in years the taste continued, but its direction was changed. He excelled in the joust and the tournament, and the dangers of an assault suited his ardent temperament. On the accession of his father to the Dukedom in 1524, he went to reside at Kenninghall, and in 1526 was appointed cupbearer to Henry the Eighth. By an extract from the register of Butley Priory, in Suffolk, it appears that on the 23rd of July, 1529, the Duke of Norfolk paid a visit to Thomas Manning (alias Sudbury) the prior of that house, accompanied by the Earl of Surrey, who is described as having then his own proper attendants. The occasion of the visit was the sale of Staverton Park, which the prior then bought of the Duke.

From a letter copied from the original among the papers of the Abbey of Bury, it would appear that the Earl, during his residence at Kenninghall, was in great pecuniary distress. It is written with more than common urgency to John Reeve, alias Melford, the head of a wealthy monastery, soon itself to be broken in pieces, and its treasures scattered to the winds.

" My Lord,
" Notwithstanding that aforetime I have borrowed of you to the sum of xxx^{li} pound sterling,

having not yet repaid it, yet by very need and
extreme necessity, I am again constrained, my
known good Lord, at this present, affectuously
to desire you to shew yourself so much my cor-
dial friend, as to lend some over and above xx^{li}
pound, in such haste as I may have it here
to-morrow by viii of the clock, for such is my
present need and thought [sadness]. My Lord,
for your such kindness to be shown towards [me],
it lieth not in my power to offer the like recompense. Yet, my Lord, ye shall so bind me to
be your inward and affectuall friend whiles I
live, and your money, first and last, to be
honestly repaid to you again with hearty thanks,
which if I were so ingrate (which God defend!)
to deny ye, might and may it well believe, my
Lord, my father will not so see your hearty
kindness uncontented. And thus, my very good
Lord, with hearty request of this my desire I
leave you to God. Displease you not so, though
my Lord being out of the country in this my
necessity, I rather attempt to assay [prove] you
his ancient friend than other farther off. From
Kenninghall, this St. Peter's, yours assuredly
during his life.   " H. SURREY.

" To his very good Lord and Friend, my
Lord Abbot of Birry give these."
    Endorsed : " My Lord of Surre xx^{li}, and be-
sides that xxx^{li}."[1]

On the 13th of February, 1532, Surrey, now

[1] Addit. MS. Brit. Museum, No. 24,493, fol. 234.

in his sixteenth year, was contracted in marriage to Lady Frances Vere, daughter of John, the fifteenth Earl of Oxford. They were married at Pentecost of the same year, but probably did not live together till about the spring of 1535.

In the month of October, 1532, when Henry VIII. went to France, in order to hold an interview with Francis I, he was attended by many of his peers, and among them the Duke of Richmond and the Earl of Surrey. " The xj. day of October Henry the Eighth, Kynge of England, landed at Caleis, with the Duke of Richmond, his bastard sonne, the Duke of Norfolke, lorde tresorer of England, the Erle of Surrey," etc.[1] After the royal conference the Duke of Richmond, accompanied by Surrey, proceeded to Paris, to prosecute their studies, where they remained for nearly twelve months. " In 1533, the xxv. of September, the Duke of Richmond, bastard sonne of King Henry the Eighth, and the Erle of Surrey, came to Caleys owt of Fraunce, where they had been almoste xij monthes."[2] During their residence at the French court, it appears they returned to England for a few weeks, for it is stated that the Earl of Surrey carried the fourth sword at the coronation of Queen Anne Boleyn in June, 1533. On May 17, 1534, the Duke of Richmond is recorded to have been the sovereign's lieutenant at the feast of the Order of the Garter kept at Windsor.

[1] *The Chronicle of Calais*, p. 41, 1846, printed for the Camden Society.   [2] Ibid. p. 164.

After the coronation the young Queen used
her influence in promoting the marriage of the
Duke of Richmond with Lady Mary Howard,
Surrey's only sister; and the King, with whom
the Howards were then in high favour, cordially
assented to the match. As the parties were related within the forbidden degrees of consanguin-
ity, a dispensation was indispensable. The young
Duke was placed at Windsor, whilst his bride
continued to live with her father. It was at
this time that Surrey again became the companion of " a king's son," as he describes himself in that beautiful poem which he wrote some
years after, during a temporary confinement in
Windsor Castle. Speaking of this period of his
life, he says :—

> " Proud Windsor, where I, in lust and joy,
> With a King's son, my childish years did pass,
> In greater feast than Priam's sons of Troy.
> Where each sweet place returns a taste full sour,
> The large green courts, where we were wont to hove,
> With eyes cast up into the Maiden's tower,
> And easy sighs, such as folk draw in love.
> The stately seats, the ladies bright of hue.
> The dances short, long tales of great delight;
> With words and looks that tigers could but rue;
> Where each of us did plead the other's right." [1]

On the 10th of March, 1536, Surrey's eldest
son Thomas was born, and his nativity, calcu-
lated by the Earl's direction, still exists; and,
which is somewhat singular, foretold some un-
defined misfortune to the father. On the 18th
of October following, he received the honour of

[1] See p. 19.

knighthood, and soon afterwards took a con-
spicuous part in public affairs.   At the trial of
his kinswoman, the unfortunate Anne Boleyn,
he was present as the representative of the Earl
Marshal, his father having presided by virtue
of his office of Lord Treasurer.   Within a few
months of her execution the tyrannical disposition of Henry the Eighth was manifested towards
Surrey's uncle, Lord Thomas Howard, who was
committed to the Tower for having married the
Lady Margaret Douglas without the King's
permission.   After being confined for two years
he died of a broken heart, an event which made
a deep impression upon the poet, who adverts to
it in one of his poems.[1]

But he experienced a heavier calamity on the
22nd of July of the same year by the death of
his friend and brother-in-law, the Duke of Richmond, of whom he speaks with the greatest
affection in a poem written some time after his
decease.[2]

It is here necessary to advert to Surrey's
supposititious passion for the fair Geraldine, his
affection for whom takes rank in the chronicles
of love with those of Abelard and Heloise, of
Petrarch and Laura, of Tasso and Leonora.
This circumstance has imparted a romantic interest to his life ; but his love for Geraldine can
only be regarded as a poetical exaggeration—an
affection of the imagination—the day-dream of
an ardent fancy.

Many of his biographers have considered that

[1] See p. 50.   [2] See p. 20.

the lady thus designated was the object of a real attachment, and so strongly was Dr. Nott impressed with this opinion, that he has ventured to place an address to Geraldine as the title of nearly all the Earl's sonnets, not only without any authority, but in contradiction to the first and every other edition of his works. This gratuitous assumption has led that writer into serious errors, and has deemed many lines in various poems to be illustrative of the history of Surrey's passion for Geraldine, which evidently refer to a different person.

One poem, and one poem only, can, upon anything like evidence, be supposed to have been addressed to the lady mentioned by the name of Geraldine :—

" From Tuscane came my Lady's worthy race." [1]

It was not till the year 1750 that any attempt was made to identify this celebrated woman ; that is, to name a lady of the family of Fitzgerald in whom met all the circumstances which surrounded the Earl of Surrey's Geraldine. In that year poor Collins published " A Supplement to the Four Volumes of the Peerage of England," containing an account of the Fitzgerald family. There, in speaking of the issue of Gerald, the ninth Earl of Kildare, he states that he married first a daughter of Lord Zouch of Codnor, by whom he had a numerous issue, which lady died on October 6, 1517 ; and in 1519 he married, secondly, Lady Margaret Gray,

[1] See p. 13.

fourth daughter of Thomas, Marquis of Dorset, by whom he had two sons and three daughters. He then states, without any reserve, that Lady Elizabeth, the second of these three daughters, was the lady who was the Geraldine of the Earl of Surrey.

A few years after, the attention of Horace Walpole was directed to this question, and he came, by his own independent consideration, to the same conclusion at which Collins had arrived, and which he announced, in 1758, in his " Catalogue of Royal and Noble Authors." He gives a kind of proof by comparison of what Surrey has told us, with what is known of Lady Elizabeth Fitzgerald, namely the Tuscan descent of Geraldine, the Irish Earl, the mother of royal extraction, her being first seen at Hunsdon, which was a nursery of the princesses Mary and Elizabeth, with whom it is probable she was brought up; that he fell in love with her at Hampton, and was separated from her by his residence at Windsor.

If we are to suppose that Surrey's passion is to be taken as a reality, and not merely a poet's fiction, we shall find the subject perplexed with difficulties. The Lady Elizabeth was a mere child, not more than twelve years old. Surrey was then married, and, for aught that appears to the contrary, was living happily with his wife, whose birth was equal to his own. It betrays too little sagacity to suppose that a young married nobleman would have publicly avowed a passion for the daughter of a powerful earl, connected with the highest families in the realm, and who was then living under the especial protection of her cousin the Princess Mary.

It is remarkable, that, whilst so extravagant a deduction has been drawn from one solitary sonnet, no notice has been hitherto taken of a poem, " The Complaint of the absence of her Lover, being upon the Sea," which bears striking marks of being dictated by the affection which subsisted between him and his Countess.[1]

Connected with the story of Surrey's vaunted affection for Geraldine is that absurd fable of his travels in Italy, to proclaim, in the true spirit of chivalry, the unparalleled charms of his mistress, and to defend the cause of her beauty with the weapons of knight errantry. The whole legend first appeared in a work entitled, " The Unfortunate Traveller, or Life of Jack Wilton," written by the notable Thomas Nash, and published in 1594. It has since been credited and endorsed by Drayton, Winstanley, Anthony à Wood, Cibber, Walpole, and Warton; but finally exploded by Dr. Nott, who has demonstrated that this famed tournament is a fiction, and that Surrey was never in Italy.

On the 12th of November, 1537, Surrey attended, as one of the principal mourners, the funeral procession of Queen Anne Seymour from Hampton to Windsor, for interment in St. George's Chapel. He was also present at court on the following New Year's Day, and presented the king with three gilt bowls and a

[1] See pp. 28-31.

cover. It was early in the year 1539, when the negociations were commencing for the matrimonial treaty between Henry VIII. and Anne of Cleves, that the following amusing colloquy took place between George Constantyne and John Barlow, Dean of Westbury, respecting the gallant Surrey, now in the twenty-second year of his age.

"*George.* If there should be any pledges sent into Cleves, in good faith I would the Earl of Surrey should be one of them.

"*Dean.* It is the most foolish proud boy that is in England.

"*George.* What, man, he hath a wife and a child, and ye call him boy?

"*Dean.* By God's mercy methink he exceedeth.

"*George.* What then? he is wise for all that, as I hear. And as for pride, experience will correct well enough. No marvel though a young man, so noble a man's son and heir apparent be proud, for we be too proud ourselves without those qualities. But I would wish that he should be one to be sent thither, for that he should there be fully instructed in God's word and of experience. For if the Duke of Norfolk were as fully persuaded in it as he is in the contrary, he should do much good, for he is an earnest man, a bold man and witty, in all his matters.

"*Dean.* It is true, and ye say well in that."[1]

In the spring of 1539 Surrey's second son,

[1] *Archæologia*, vol. xxiii. p. 62.

Henry, afterwards created Earl of Northampton, was born, and it is clear that our poet at this time maintained the state and dignity of a nobleman in everything.   Hence we find him on the 1st of May, 1540, with the knightly gallants of the court, distinguishing himself at the jousts and tournaments held at Durham House in honour of the king's marriage with Anne of Cleves, " where he behaved himself with admirable courage, and great skill in the use of his arms."[1]   Towards the close of that year Surrey accompanied the forces which were sent to put Guisnes into a state of defence, in case of a rupture with France, when he commenced his military career;   his stay there was, however, very short.

Early in 1541, Sir Edmund Knevett struck the Earl's friend and attendant, Thomas Clere, within the precincts of the court.   For this offence the usual punishment of the loss of the right hand was pronounced; but at Surrey's intercession, according to Dr. Nott, Knevett was pardoned.   Hollingshed, however, says that Knevett obtained the king's grace himself, by begging that his left hand might be taken, and his right spared to render future service to his majesty.   In September of the same year, Surrey and his father were appointed Stewards of the University of Cambridge.

On February 12th, 1542, the second of the five queens of Henry the Eighth, Catherine Howard, was sent to the block in the Tower;

[1] Dugdale's *Baronage*, ii. 275.

but as a proof that the king still cherished some regard for the queen's family, on St. George's day of the same year Surrey received one of the highest favours which his sovereign could confer, by being elected a Knight of the Garter.

Peculiarly susceptible of affront or injury, Surrey never hesitated a moment in resenting whatever appeared to affect his honour. A few months afterwards we find him again involved in a quarrel with a gentleman of the name of John à Leigh, whom he challenged, and the dispute has, without a shadow of proof, been attributed by Dr. Nott to Leigh's being his rival in Geraldine's affections! Be the cause, however, what it might, Surrey was evidently in fault, for he was sent a prisoner to the Fleet, being allowed two servants to attend upon him, but not permitted to entertain any friends at his table. The following letter was written during his confinement, and is of much interest. It was addressed to the Privy Council, and entreated them to obtain his liberation, or at least to intercede that he might be removed to a less noisome prison :—

" MY VERY GOOD LORDS,

" After my humble commendations to your Lordships; these presents shall be to advertise you, that albeit I have of late severally required each of you, by my servant Pickering, of your favour; from whom as yet I have received no other comfort than my passed folly hath deserved; I have yet thought it my duty again, as

well to renew my suit, as humbly to require you
rather to impute this error to the fury of reckless
youth, than to a will not conformable and contented, with the quiet learning of the just reward
of my folly; for as much as I so suddenly and
quickly did procure and attempt to seek for
friendship, and entreat for my deliverence: as
then not sufficiently pondering nor debating with
myself, that a prince offended hath none redress
upon his subject but condign punishment, without respect of person.   Yet, let my youth un-
practised in durance obtain pardon: (although
for lack of strength it yield not itself wholly to
his gentle chastisement,) whilst the heart is resolved in patience to pass over the same, in satis-
faction of mine errors.

   " And, my Lords, if it were lawful to persuade
by the precedent of other young men reconciled,
I would affirm that this might sound to me a
happy fault: by so gentle a warning to learn
how to bridle my heady will: which in youth is
rarely attained without adversity.   Where, might
I without vaunt lay before you the quiet conversation of my passed life; which (unstained
with any unhonest touch, unseeming in such a
man as it hath pleased God and the King to
make me,) might perfectly promise new amend-
ment of mine offence.   Whereof, if you doubt
in any point, I shall humbly desire you, that
during mine affliction, (in which time malice is
most ready to slander the innocent) there may
be made an whole examination of my life:
wishing, for the better trial thereof, to have the

time of my durance redoubled; and so (declared
as well tried, and unsuspected) by your media-
tions to be restored to the King's favour; than,
condemned in your grave heads, without answer
or further examination to be quickly delivered:
this heinous offence always unexcused, whereupon I was committed to this noisome prison;
whose pestilent airs are not unlike to bring some
alteration of health.

" Wherefore, if your good Lordships judge
me not a member rather to be clean cut away,
than reformed; it may please you to be suitors
to the King's Majesty on my behalf; as well
for his favour, as for my liberty: or else, at the
least, if his pleasure be to punish this oversight
with the forbearing his presence, (which unto
every loving subject, specially unto me, from a
Prince cannot be less counted than a living
death,) yet it would please him to command me
into the country, to some place of open air, with
like restraint of liberty, there to abide his Grace's
pleasure.

" Finally, albeit no part of this my trespass in
any way to do me good, I should judge me
happy if it should please the King's Majesty to
think, that this simple body rashly adventured
in the revenge of his own quarrel, shall be without respect always ready to be employed in his
service; trusting once so to redouble this error,
which may be well repeated but not revoked.
Desiring your good Lordships that like as my
offence hath not been, my submission may likewise appear: which is all the recompense that I

may well think my doings answer not. Your grave heads should yet consider, that neither am I the first young man that hath enterprised such things as he hath afterward repented."

He continued a prisoner until the 7th of August, when he was released upon his recognizance in ten thousand marks not to offer any further offence, by word or deed, to Leigh or to any of his friends. War being soon afterwards declared against Scotland, Lord Surrey accompanied the expedition into that kingdom under his father, the Duke of Norfolk, but it is not known what rank he bore in the army. It is evident, from his epitaph on his friend Clere, that he was present at the burning of Kelsal, but on breaking up the English forces soon afterwards, the Earl returned to London.

An affair occurred early in the year 1543 which is remarkable for two reasons, the one as proving the impetuosity of Surrey's temper; the other that he was at this time encouraging perilous expectations respecting the anticipated regency, as the health of the king was rapidly declining. A party of gentlemen, of whom Surrey was one, amused the long hours of a winter night by a riot in London. They paraded the streets with stone bows, they broke the windows of houses and churches, shot pellets among the queans upon the Bankside, and then disappeared among the unlighted alleys of the city. In the morning they were traced to the house of a Master Arundel in Laurence Lane.

The rank of the offenders led to an inquiry by the Privy Council, and the examination of the witnesses, especially of Mrs. Arundel's servants, showed that Surrey allowed himself to be regarded by his friends as more than the hero of a midnight disturbance.[1]

On the 1st of April, 1543, the Earl was summoned before the Privy Council, and charged with two offences: having eaten flesh in Lent, and having walked about the streets of the city at night in a " lewd and unseemly manner," and breaking several windows with a stone bow. To the first charge he replied, that he had a license; but to the latter he pleaded guilty, and submitted himself to such punishment as might be thought proper, whereupon he was again sent to the

[1] Froude's *History of England,* iv. 252, where is also printed from the MS. State Paper Office, Domestic, vol. xiv. the following examination of Mistress Arundel. She said, "that the Earl of Surrey and other young noblemen frequented her house, eating meat in Lent, and committing other improprieties. Further, she saith, how at Candlemas they went out with stone bows at nine o'clock at night, and did not come back till past midnight, and the next day there was a great clamour of the breaking of many glass windows both of houses and churches, and shooting at men that night in the street; and the voice was that those hurts were done by my Lord and his company. Whereupon she gave commandment unto all her house that they should say nothing of my Lord's going out in form specified. Item, she said, that that night, or the night before, they used the same stone bows, rowing on the Thames; and Thomas Cleer told her how they shot at the queans on the Bankside. Mistress Arundel also, looking one day at Lord Surrey's arms, said the arms were very like the King's arms; and said further, she thought he would be King, if aught but good happened to the King and Prince."

Fleet.[1] During his confinement Surrey grati-
fied his spleen against the citizens, whose complaint produced his imprisonment, by giving an
account of the transaction in the poem entitled,
" A Satire against the Citizens of London,"[2] in
which he wittily says that his conduct was intended as a punishment for their crimes. His
companions in the outrage, Pickering and the
young Wyatt, were also both sent to prison: the
former to the Porter's Lodge, and the latter to
the Counter.

Surrey's imprisonment was of short duration,
for in October following his father sent him to
Sir John Wallop, the commander of the army
with which Henry had assisted the Emperor.
He joined the allied camp before Landrecy, near
Boulogne, being attended by his faithful servants Clere and Blage. Wallop thus announced
his arrival to the king :—

" Yesterday Blage, who arrived here with my
Lord of Surrey, went with Mr. Carew to see the
trench, and escaped very hardly from a piece of
ordnance that was shot towards him. My said
Lord I brought about a great part of the town
to view the same ; and in his return was somewhat saluted. Their powder and shot they do
bestow amongst us plentifully, and sometime doth
hurt. My said Lord's coming unto this camp
was very agreeable unto the Duke, and great
Master, declaring a great amity and friendship
that your Majesty beareth to the Emperor. I

[1] Privy Council Book of the Reign of Henry VIII.
[2] See page 68.

was very glad that my said Lord intended to go unto Fernando's camp, informing him, as they offered him sufficient conduct, and the great Master himself to bring him half way there."

In various letters from Sir John Wallop, Surrey's assiduity and skill in acquiring military knowledge are mentioned in terms of the highest panegyric. The siege was raised early in November, and, the army having gone into winter quarters, the Earl returned to England. It is supposed that he employed himself for some time afterwards in constructing his beautiful seat of Mount Surrey, at St. Leonard's, near Norwich, on the site of an ancient cell of Benedictine friars.

It was about the time when Surrey was engaged in finishing his magnificent building that he received into his family the celebrated Hadrian Junius as a physician, assigning him apartments at Kenninghall, with a yearly salary of fifty angels. Near this time, too, the poet Churchyard seems to have entered the Earl's service, as one of his pages, where, under the protection of such an accomplished master, he could both cultivate his music and his muse. In the following verses he paints Surrey's talents and virtues in glowing colours, rejoicing that he was for four years one of his retainers :—

" A master of no mean estate, a mirror in those days,
His happy fortune then him gat, whose virtues must I praise.
More heavenly were those gifts he had than earthly was his
    form,

c

His corpse too worthy for the grave, his flesh no meat for
    worm.
An Earl of birth; a God of sprite, a Tully for his tongue;
Methink of right the world should shake when half his praise
    were rung.
Oh! cursed were those crooked crafts, that his own country
    wrought
To chop off such a chosen head as our time ne'er forth brought.
His knowledge crept beyond the stars and wrought to Jove's
    high throne,
The bowels of the earth he saw, in his deep breast y-known.
His wit looked through each man's device; his judgment
    grounded was,
Almost he had foresight to know ere things should come to
    pass;
When they should fall; what should betide, Oh! what a
    loss of weight
Was it to lose so ripe a head, that reached to such height!
In every heart he feeling had : with pen past Petrarch sure,
A fashion framed which could his foes to friendship oft allure,
His virtues could not keep him here, but rather wrought his
    harms,
And made his enemies murmur oft, and brought them in by
    swarms.
Whose practice put him to his plunge, and lost his life thereby,
Oh! canker'd breasts which have such hearts wherein such
    hate doth lie.
As I have told this young man served this master twice two
    year,
And learned therein such fruitful skill, as long he held full
    dear.
And used the pen as he was taught and other gifts also,
Which made him hold the cap on head, where some do crouch
    full low."

About July, 1544, Henry again invaded
France with a large army, the vanguard of
which was commanded by the Duke of Norfolk,
and Surrey was appointed Marshal, an office of
considerable importance, and requiring capacity
and courage. The van and rearguard having
joined the Emperor's forces, they laid siege to

Montreuil, and on the 26th of July, Henry invested Boulogne in person. As that town was the principal object of the King's attention all the resources were bestowed upon the besiegers, and his troops before Montreuil were allowed to want ammunition and pay. Norfolk's exertions did not, however, relax; and, aided by his son, he succeeded in distressing the garrison by famine. Surrey more than once distinguished himself during the siege, and his services are thus mentioned in one of his father's dispatches:—

" With hearty recommendations this shall be to advertise your good Lordships that this evening Monsieur de Bewers with his band, and my son of Surrey, my Lord of Sussex, my Lord Mountjoy, my brother William, my Lord Latimer, Mr. Treasurer, and all the rest of the noblemen whom I sent further upon Saturday at ten at night, returned hither to this camp this night at seven o'clock, without loss of any man slain, and have made a very honest journey, and have burnt the towns of St. Riquier and Riew, both walled towns, and also the fauxbourg of Abbeville, on this side of the town, where the English horsemen had a right hot skirmish, and after the coming of the whole army retired without loss, and burned all the country; and they of Crotey fearing our men would have laid siege of the castle, burned their own town. Our men have brought a very great booty of all sorts of cattle; the noblemen and gentlemen kept their footmen in such order, that they borrowed nothing of the Burgonians, and finally have made

such an excourse, that the like hath not been
made since these wars began."

In an attempt to storm Montreuil on the 19th
of September, the Earl was either wounded or
much exhausted, and he owed his life to the
fidelity of Clere, who in bringing him off received a hurt which eventually caused his death.
This affecting incident Surrey has himself com-
memorated in his epitaph on Clere:—

> " Tracing whose steps thou sawest Kelsal blaze,
> Landrecy burnt, and batter'd Boulogne render.
> At Montreuil gates, hopeless of all recure,
> Thine Earl, half dead, gave in thy hand his will;
> Which cause did thee this pining death procure." [1]

On the 25th of September a reinforcement
was sent to the Duke of Norfolk, but it arrived
too late: the siege of Montreuil was raised, and
the English army retired to Boulogne on the
30th of that month. Norfolk reached England
about the middle of December, and as nothing
further is recorded of Surrey until Christmas
Day, when he attended a Chapter of the Garter
at Hampton Court, it may be inferred that he
came back with his father. According to Monsieur Du Bellay, Surrey was again at Boulogne
soon afterwards, but this statement is doubtful,
and it is certain that he was present at a Chapter
of the Garter on St. George's Day in 1545.

In July following he was at Kenninghall, in
Norfolk, where he received a letter from the
Privy Council respecting some men that were
raised for the expedition for the defence of Bou-

[1] See p. 62.

logne, which was then menaced by the French.
The Earl was appointed commander of the vanguard, consisting of five thousand soldiers, with
which he arrived at Calais in August, where he
was joined by three thousand.   On the 26th of
that month he was constituted Commander of
Guisnes; but within a short time he was removed, at his own request, to Boulogne.   The
post of Commander of Boulogne required energy,
courage, and skill, and there is ample evidence
that the Earl displayed each of those qualifica-
tions.   Many of his despatches describing the
state of affairs at different times are extant, but
they contain little of general interest.   A letter
from his father to him, written in September,
justifies the inference that his representations to
the King, urging him to retain Boulogne, were
not agreeable to the Privy Council :—

" TO MY SON OF SURREY.

" WITH this ye shall receive your letter sent to
me by this bearer; by the which I perceive ye
find yourself grieved for that I declared to the
King such things as Cavendish shewed to me:
which I did by his desire; shewing the same of
his behalf without speaking of you.   And if he
will say he desired not me to shew the King
thereof, ye may [say] he sayeth untruly.   For
the King hawking for a pheasant, he desired me
as he went homeward to declare the same to his
Highness.   This is true, and he taken here not
of the best sort.   Ye may be sure I do not use
my doings of any sort that may turn you to any

displeasure. Have yourself in await, that ye animate not the King too much for the keeping of Boulogne; for who so doth, at length shall get small thanks. I have so handled the matter, that if any adventure be given to win the new fortress at Boulogne, ye shall have the charge thereof; and therefore, look well what answer ye make to the letter from us of the Council. Confirm not the enterprises contained in them.

" Having written the premises, Mr. Paget desired me to write to you in no wise to animate the King to keep Boulogne. Upon what grounds he spake it I know not; but I fear ye wrote something too much therein to somebody. And thus with God's blessing and mine, Fare ye well. From Windsor, the 27th of September at night.

" Your loving father,

" T. NORFOLK."

In a postscript to an unimportant letter to Lord Cobham, dated at Boulogne on the 20th of October, 1545, Surrey says,—

" Whereas, I perceive Sir Edward Wotton's son fantaseth a genet gelding of mine, that standeth at Calais, which is blind and winded, I am ashamed to give him; but if it please him to take him till I be able to give him a better, I shall desire him so to do."

A communication addressed to Sir William Paget, on the 20th of the following month, will be inserted, as it shews the zeal with which the Earl advocated the interests of his friends :—

" It may like you, gentle Mr. Secretary, to give me leave, amid your weighty affairs, to trouble you with an earnest suit. Whereas Mr. Treasurer of Guisnes is discharged, and some other, as I hear, appointed to his place, it will please you to inform yourself by the report of such as knoweth, [of] a gentleman, sometime my servant, and now a captain within this town, called T. Shelley, what his conditions and qualities are, and disposition to service, and then to square within yourself whether it be meet to recommend for that office such one, at the most effectual request of your poor friend, of whose rare virtues I could write more at large, but that I know virtue for the self, is to you sufficiently recommended; and that Mr. Palmer awaiteth upon you, who can sufficiently of the ability of the man instruct you. Assuring you, Sir, that I dare promise more of that man, his truth and honesty, than of any man that I know alive; and I should think myself happy to have bred such a servant, as I trust his Majesty should find him. And for your favour to be granted that man, I shall most heartily beseech you, and think the pleasure done as to myself, praying you to pardon my earnest writing: for the worthiness of the man bears it. And thus leaving to trouble you, I pray to God to send you health. From Boulogne, the 20th of November.

" Your own most assuredly,

" H. SURREY."

Surrey having received intimation early in
January, 1545-6, that the French were about
to advance from Montreuil to re-victual the
fortress, he marched from Boulogne with great
part of the garrison to intercept them near St.
Etienne. Though he was inferior in numbers,
he gallantly attacked the French troops; but,
in consequence of the cowardice of one division
of his forces, who fled in confusion, notwithstanding all the Earl's efforts to rally them, the
English were defeated, and forced to retreat to
Boulogne.

Surrey's despatch to the King, giving an
account of this affair, is as follows :—

" It may like your most excellent Majesty;
that having certain espial that Monsieur Du
Biez was set fort [forth] of Montreuil with six
hundred horse, and three thousand footmen, to
relieve the great necessity of the fortress, mentioned in our former letters; we took yesterday
before day the trenches at St. Etienne, with six
hundred footmen, and sent out Mr. Ellerkar
with all the horsemen of this town, and Mr.
Pollard with two hundred, that he brought the
night before from Guisnes, to discover whither
their camp marched, which he had discovered
by their fires at Nouclier over night, six miles
on this side Montreuil. And as they passed by
Hardelot, Mr. Pollard was hurt with a culverin
in the knee, and died thereof the night following;
of whom your Majesty had a notable loss.

"Our horsemen discovered their march beyond
Hardelot, whereupon I, the Earl of Surrey, being

advertised, according to the order agreed upon
amongst us, issued out with Mr. Bridges, Sir
Henry Palmer, Sir Thomas Palmer, Sir Thomas
Wyatt, and two thousand footmen; leaving within
your Majesty's pieces two thousand footmen, and
the rest of the council here, divided in the pieces.
And by that time that we had set our horsemen
and footmen in order of battle, without the trench
of St. Etienne, the enemy was also in order of
battle on this side Hardelot, and had put on
their carriages by the sea's side, towards the fortress. Whereupon, having discovered their horsemen not above five hundred, and footmen about
four thousand, pondering the weight of the service, which might have imported no less success
than the winning of the fortress ; and the courage
and good will that seemed in our men (the surety
of your Majesty's pieces being provided for) upon
a consultation we presented them the fight with
a squadre of pikes and bills, about threescore in
file, and two wings of harquebussiers, and one
of bows ; and our horsemen on the right wing.
Many of the captains and gentlemen were in the
first rank by their desire; for because they were
well armed in corselets. The battle of the Almains came towards us likewise with two wings
of harquebussiers and two troops of horsemen.

" Mr. Marshall, Mr. Bellingham, Mr. Porter,
Mr. Shelley, and Mr. Granado, with all the
horsemen of this town, and Guisnes, gave the
charge upon their right flank, and brake their
harquebussiers. Their horsemen fled and ours
followed the victory, and killed and slew till they

came to the carriages, where they brake four
score and ten, accompted by tale this morning.
Our squadre then joined with the Almains, with
a cry of as great courage, and in as good order
as we could wish.   And by that time our first
rank and the second were come to the push of
the pike, there grew a disorder in our men, and
without cause fled; at which time many of our
gentlemen were slain, which gave as hardy an
onset as hath been seen, and could but have
had good success, if they had been followed.
So, stinted they never for any devise that we
could use, till they came to the trenches : and
being well settled there, which is such a place as
may be kept against all their camp, they forsook
that and took the river, which gave the enemy
courage to follow them : albeit the night drawing
then on, they followed not far beyond.   Assuring
your Majesty that the fury of their flight was such,
that it booted little the travail that was taken
upon every strait to stay them.   And so seeing
it not possible to stop them, we suffered them to
retire to the town.   In this meanwhile, our horsemen thinking all won, finding the disorder, were
fain to pass over at a passage a mile beneath
Pont de Brique, without any loss, having slain
a great number of the enemies ; whereof we have
yet no certain advertisement.

"Thus was there loss and victory on both
sides.   And this morning we sent over afore day
to number the dead.   There was slain of our
side two hundred and five ; whereof captains
Mr. Edward Poynings, Captain Story, Captain
Jones, Spencer, Roberts, Basford, Wourth,

Wynchcombe, Mr. Vawse, and a man at arms
called Harvy.   Captain Crayford and Mr. John
Palmer, and Captain Shelley, and Captain Cobham, missed, but not found. All these were slain
in the first rank.   Other there were that escaped.
Among whom Mr. Wyatt was one; assuring
your Majesty that there were never gentlemen
served more hardily, if it had chanced, and saving
the disorder of our footmen that fled without
cause, when all things almost seemed won.   The
enemy took more loss than we, but for the gentlemen ; whose loss was much to be lamented.
And this day we have kept the field from the
break of day ; and the enemy retired to Montreuil
immediately after the fight, and left their carriages distressed behind them.   And not twenty
carts entered into the fortress; and that biscuit.

" Beseeching your Majesty, though the success
hath not been such as we wished, to accept the
good intent of us all ; considering that it seemed
to us, in a matter of such importance, a necessary
thing to present the fight.   And that Mr. Ellerkar may know we have humbly recommended
his good service unto your Highness ; which was
such, as if all the rest had answered to the same,
the enemy had been utterly discomforted; and
that it may please your Majesty to give him
credit for the declaration thereof more at large.
Further; whereas Mr. Henry Dudley was one
of those of the first rank that gave the onset
upon the enemy, and is a man [to be esteemed]
for his knowledge, heart, and of good service, it
may like your Highness to be his good and gracious Lord ; that whereas Mr. Poynings, late

captain of your Majesty's guard here is deceased, if your Highness shall think him able to succeed him in that room, at our humble intercession to admit him thereto; if it may so stand with your most gracious pleasure.

" And thus beseeching your Highness to accept our poor service, albeit the success in all things was not such as we wished, yet was the enemies enterprise disappointed, which could not have been otherwise done, and more of their part slain than of ours; and the fortress in as great misery as before, and a sudden flight the let of a full victory. And if any disorder there were, we assure your Majesty there was no default in the rulers, nor lack of courage to be given them, but a humour that sometime reigneth in Englishmen: most humbly thanking your Majesty that it hath pleased the same to consider their payment; which shall much revive their hearts to adventure most willingly their lives, according to their most bounden duty, in your Majesty's service, to make recompense for the disorder that now they have made.

" And thus we pray to God to preserve your most excellent Majesty. From your Highness's town of Boulogne, this 8th of January, 1546.

Your Majesty's most humble
and obedient Servants and Subjects,

H. SURREY.

HUGH POULET.   HENRY PALMER.

RICHARD CAVENDISH.   JOHN BYRGGYS.

RICHARD WYNDEBANCKE.

" P.S. Whereas we think that this victual can
serve for no long time, that they have put into
the fortress; wherefore it is to be thought the
enemy will attempt the like again shortly: it
may please your Majesty to resolve what is further to be done by us; and for the declaration
of our poor opinions therein, we have sent Mr.
Ellerkar to your Majesty, to whom may it please
your Highness to give credit in that behalf; and
the present tempest being such, we have thought
it meet to send these before, and stay him for a
better passage."

His defeat has been supposed to have lessened
the good opinion which the King entertained of
him; but this is doubtful, as he continued in the
command of Boulogne for three months after
that event; and, in the beginning of March,
he applied to Henry for permission that his wife
might join him at Boulogne, which request was
refused, on the ground that " time of service,
which will bring some trouble and disquietness
unmeet for women's imbecilities, approacheth."
The first intimation he received that he was to
be superseded was in a letter from Secretary
Paget, dated about the middle of March, in
which there are these passages :—

" My Lord, the latter part of your letter,
touching the intended enterprise of the enemy,
giveth me occasion to write unto you frankly my
poor opinion; trusting your Lordship will take
the same in no worse part than I mean it. As
your Lordship wisheth, so his Majesty mindeth
to do somewhat for the endommaging of the

enemy : and for that purpose hath appointed to
send an army over shortly, and that my Lord of
Hertford shall be his Highness's Lieutenant
General at his being in Boulonnois.[1]   Whereby
I fear your authority of Lieutenant shall be
touched : for I believe that the later ordering of
a Lieutenant taketh away the commission of
him that was there before.   Now, my Lord, because you have been pleased I should write mine
advice to your Lordship in things concerning
your honour and benefit, I could no less do than
put you in remembrance how much in mine
opinion this shall touch your honour, if you
should pass the thing over in silence until the
very time of my Lord of Hertford's coming over
thither ; for so should both your authority be
taken away, as I fear is Boulonnois, and also it
should fortune ye to come abroad without any
place of estimation in the field ; which the world
would much muse at, and, though there be no
such matter, think you were rejected upon occasion of some either negligence, inexperience, or
such other like fault ; for so many heads so
many judgments.   Wherefore, my Lord, in my
opinion, you should do well to make sure by
times to his Majesty to appoint you to some
place of service in the army ; as to the Captain-
ship of the Foreward, or Rearward ; or to such
other place of honour as should be meet for you ;

---

[1] This appointment was announced officially by the Privy
Council to Surrey and the Council of Boulogne on the 21st
of March, 1545-6, by a dispatch of which a minute is in the
State Paper Office, and has been printed by Nott, i. 227.
Lord Hertford reached Calais on the 23rd of March.

for so should you be where knowledge and experience may be gotten. Whereby you should
the better be able hereafter to serve, and also to
have peradventure occasion to do some notable
service in revenge of your men, at the last encounter with the enemies, which should be to
your reputation in the world. Whereas, being
hitherto noted as you are a man of a noble courage, and of a desire to show the same to the
face of your enemies, if you should now tarry at
home within a wall, having I doubt a show of
your authority touched, it would be thought
abroad I fear, that either you were desirous to
tarry in a sure place of rest, or else that the
credit of your courage and forwardness to serve
were diminished; and that you were taken here
for a man of [little] activity or service.

" Wherefore, in my opinion, you shall do well,
and provide wisely for the conservation of your
reputation, to sue to his Majesty for a place of
service in the field. Wherein if it shall please
you to use me as a mean to his Majesty, I trust
so to set forth the matter to his Majesty, as he
shall take the same in gracious part, and be
content to appoint you to such a place as may
best stand with your honour. And this counsel
I write unto you as one that would you well;
trusting that your Lordship will even so inter-
pret the same, and let me know your mind here-
in betimes."

Within a few weeks Surrey was summoned to
the King's presence to advise on the best mode
of fortifying Boulogne; but this command was

in fact a civil manner of announcing that he was superseded by the Earl of Hertford.

The next notice which occurs of the Earl is the following letter from him to Secretary Paget, dated on the 14th of July, which is very cha racteristic. It relates to his conduct whilst com mander of Boulogne with respect to the claims of some of the King's servants, as well as of persons to whom Surrey had given certain appointments. His reply to Lord Grey's insinuation that he had himself derived a profit from them is written with all the dignity of conscious integrity: "There are," he says, "in Boulogne too many witnesses that Henry of Surrey was never corrupted by personal considerations, and that his hand never closed upon a bribe: a lesson," he adds, "which he learnt from his father, whom he desired to imitate in this as in all other things."

" To the Right Worshipful Sir William Paget, Kt. one of his Majesty's Principal Secretaries:

" It may like you, with my hearty commendations; that whereas yesternight I perceived by you, that the King's Majesty thinketh his liberality sufficiently extended towards the strangers that have served him, I have with fair words done my best so to satisfy them accordingly; assuring you on my faith, that their necessity seemed to me such, as it cost me an hundred ducats of mine own purse, and somewhat else:

so that now there resteth nothing to be done but
their passports and ready dispatch from you,
wherein it may please you to consider their
great charges here.

" And now you shall give me leave to come
to mine own matters. Coming from Boulogne
in such sort as you know, I left only two of my
servants behind me; John Rosington and Thomas Copeland. To the said John, for his notable service, I gave the advantage of the play in
Boulogne; to Thomas, the prefect of the passage: whom my Lord Grey put immediately
out of service after my departure, notwithstanding the letter I obtained from you to him in
their favour. Upon a better consideration, John
occupieth his room; and my Lord to his own
use occupieth the other's office of the passage;
saying, ' That I, and my predecessors there
should use the same to our gain;' (which I assure
you is untrue) and that it should be parcel of
the entertainment of the Deputy; which in
Calais was never used, and is, me seemeth, too
near for a Deputy to grate; unless it were for
some displeasure borne me.

" Finally, Mr. Secretary, this is the only suit
that I have made you for any thing touching
Boulogne sith my departure; wherefore it may
please you, that if my Lord Grey will needs be
passager, and that the office was no less worth
to the said Thomas than fifty pounds a year,
being placed there by a King's Lieutenant,
(which me thinketh a great disorder that a Captain of Boulogne should displace for any private

d

gain,) yet at the least it may please you to request my Lord Grey to recompense him with a
sum of money in recompense of that, that he
hath lost, and purchased so dearly with so many
dangers of life; which my said Lord of his
liberality cannot refrain to do.

" And for answer, that my said Lord chargeth
me to have returned the same to my private profit, in his so saying he can have none honour.
For there be in Boulogne too many witnesses
that Henry of Surrey was never for singular
profit corrupted; nor never yet bribe closed his
hand : which lesson I learned of my father ; and
wish to succeed him therein as in the rest.

" Further ; whereas the said Copeland was
placed there for his merits by Mr. Southwell,
and me, of the guard ; and that my said Lord
Grey detaineth from him his wages, it may please
you, at my hearty request, to grant him your
letters for the obtaining thereof; and of the rest,
and to pardon my frankness, for that you know
it is my natural, to use it with [such as I do
hold my friends]. And thus wishing you [to
continue ever more] my friend, till I deserve
of [any fault of mine the con]trary, I pray to
God send you [what ever good your own]
heart desireth. From — — — —14th July
1546.

" Your assured loving friend,

" H. Surrey."

The great influence which the Earl of Hert-

ford possessed was viewed with jealousy by Norfolk and his son, though they sought to conci-
liate him by proposing an alliance between the
widowed Duchess of Richmond, whose marriage
was never consummated, and the Earl's brother,
Sir Thomas Seymour. This alliance did not,
however, take place, and Surrey, either from dislike of Hertford or from some other cause, was not
employed under him. Disappointed ambition,
in a person of an impetuous and haughty temper,
generally vents itself in bitter speeches against
the author of a supposed wrong; and Surrey,
after his return to England, towards the end of
March, 1547, often expressed himself with great
asperity about Hertford.

This conduct having reached the king's ears,
Surrey was arrested and imprisoned at Windsor
in July following, when Henry ordered his
father to be apprised of his imprudence. The
Duke in a letter to the Council desired them to
thank his Majesty for informing him of his son's
" foolish demeanour ;" and after expressing pleasure at finding he had evinced a proper sense
of his behaviour, Norfolk prayed that he might
be " earnestly handled, in order that he may
have regard hereafter so to use himself, that he
may give his Majesty no cause of discontent."
Surrey's confinement must have been short, as
he officiated at court early in August, on the
arrival of the French Ambassadors.

During the first two weeks of December the
enemies of the Earl were actively engaged in
collecting evidence to accomplish his destruction.

The king was known to be dying, and the Earl of Hertford, as uncle to the heir of the throne, aspired to be protector of the kingdom during the minority of his nephew ; whilst on the other hand, Surrey had been for some years speculating on a Norfolk regency. Suspicion having been aroused by the assumption of the royal arms by the Earl, and his known dislike to " the new nobility," it was not difficult to contrive the mesh in which he was ultimately snared. From some fragments of evidence discovered by Mr. Froude in the State Paper Office (Domestic, vol. xix.) we have a remarkable illustration of the hastiness of Surrey's temper, and the enthusiastic turn of his mind.

" Sir Edmund Warner being commanded by Sir William Paget to put in writing all such words and communications as had heretofore been betwixt him and the Earl of Surrey that might in any wise touch the King's Highness and his posterity, or of any other person, what he had heard of the said Earl that might in any way tend to the same effect, deposed, that of the Earl himself he had heard nothing ; but in the summer last past Mr. Devereux did tell him upon certain communications of the pride and vain glory of the said Earl, that it was possible it might be abated one day ; and when he, Sir Edmund Warner, asked what he meant thereby, he said, what if he were accused to the King, that he should say, ' If God should call the King to his mercy, who were so meet to govern the Prince as my Lord his father.' "

"Sir Edward Rogers being examined, deposed, Sir George Blage was in communication
with the Earl and me, and the Earl entered in
question with Blage, or Blage with the Earl,
who were meetest to have the rule and governance of the Prince in case God should disclose
his pleasure on the King's majesty.   Blage said
he thought meetest such as his Highness should
appoint.   The Earl contrary-wise said that his
father was the meetest personage to be deputed
to that room, as well in respect of the good service he had done, as also for his estate.   Blage
answered, saying, He trusted never to see that
day, and that the Prince should be but evil
taught if he were of his father's teaching."

But a sadder charge against the character of
Surrey was next to follow, of which it is difficult
to believe it capable.

"Sir Gawin Carew examined, said that my
Lady of Richmond (sister of the Earl) had discovered unto him as strange a practice of her
brother as ever he had heard of, which was that
the aforesaid Earl, pretending the face of a marriage to have succeeded between Sir Thomas
Seymour and the said lady, did will and advise
her that what time the King's majesty should
send for her (as it should be brought about that
the King's Highness should move her in that
behalf), she should so order herself as neither
she should seem to grant nor to deny that his
Majesty did will her unto, but rather to so temper her tale as his Highness might thereby have
occasion to send for her again, and so possibly

that his Majesty might cast some love unto her,
whereby in process she should bear as great a
stroke about him as Madame d'Estampes did .
about the French king."

In another deposition on the same subject,
the deponent says, " that the reply of the Duchess to these suggestions was, that she defied
her brother, and said that they should all perish,
and she would cut her own throat rather than
she would consent to such a villany."

On the 12th of December Surrey and his
father were arrested and sent to the Tower, each
being ignorant of the other's fate, and the king
was persuaded to proceed to extremities with the
Howards. The Duchess of Richmond at this
time was at her usual residence, her father's
mansion of Kenninghall, near Thetford, whither
three commissioners, Sir John Gate, Sir Richard
Southwell, and Sir Wymound Carew, were dis-
patched in all haste. Their report to the King [1]
not only gives a graphic picture of this startling
catastrophe in a great household; but shows
how overcome with alarm and doubt the Duchess herself was, and how, in her natural anxiety
to defend her father, she was entrapped perhaps
into making further admissions respecting her
brother than she might otherwise have done.

The commissioners state, that on their arrival
at Kenninghall on December 14, 1546, " we
did declare our desire to speak with the Duchess

---

[1] Printed *in extenso* in the *State Papers, temp. Henry
VIII*, vol. i. p. 888, published by the Record Commission.

of Richmond and Elizabeth Holland, [1] both which we found at that time newly risen, and not ready. Nevertheless, having knowledge that we would speak with them, they came unto us without delay into the dining chamber, and so we imparted unto them the case and condition wherein the said Duke and his son, without your great mercy, did stand ; wherewith as we found the Duchess a woman sore perplexed, trembling, and like to fall down, so coming unto herself again, she was not, we assure your Majesty, forgetful of her duty, and did most humbly and reverently upon her knees humble herself in all unto your Highness, saying that although nature constrained her sore to love her father, whom she hath ever thought to be a true and faithful subject, and also to desire the well-doing of his son, her natural brother, whom she noteth to be a rash man. Yet, for her part, she would nor will hide or conceal any thing from your Majesty's knowledge, specially if it be of weight, or otherwise, as it shall fall in her remembrance, which she hath promised, for the better declaration of her integrity, to exhibit in writing unto your Highness's most honourable council."

The commissioners then state, that they

[1] " That drab, Bess Holland," as the enraged Duchess of Norfolk styles her in one of her letters, who was the principal cause of the domestic quarrels at Kenninghall. She retained her influence over the Duke until the time of his attainder, as is amply shown by the inventories of her apparel and jewels, which were seized by the commissioners, but afterwards restored to her.

searched the chambers and coffers of the
Duchess, but found no papers of consequence,
and her chambers were, they report, "so bare,
as your majesty will hardly think, her jewels,
such as she had, sold or lende to gage, to pay
her debts, as she, her maidens, and the almoner
do say." In Elizabeth Holland's chamber were
found more trinkets, girdles, beads, buttons,
rings, &c., but still no papers.   The Countess of
Surrey is named as being at Kenninghall with
her children and nursery women, and "looking
her time to lie in at this next Candlemass."
The King's will is consulted as to whether she is
to remain there, or the household to be broken
up.   The Duchess of Richmond and Elizabeth
Holland set off that day or the next for London.

The Earl of Surrey was accused of high treason under the statute of the 28th of Henry VIII,
chap. vii. sect. 12, entitled, "An Act for the Es-
tablishment of the Succession of the Imperial
Crown of the Realm," whereby, among other
offences, it was enacted, that if any person by
speaking, writing, or printing, or by any other
act or deed, did any thing to the peril of the
King's person or of his heir, or should by any
act, speech, or deed, occasion the King to be
disturbed in the possession of his Crown, he
should be considered a traitor.   The indictment
then proceeds to recite that King Edward the
Confessor had borne certain arms which belonged
exclusively to that monarch, his progenitors,
and successors, Kings of England; that Henry
and all his progenitors had, from time immemo-

rial, used and borne the said arms, they being
annexed to the crown of England; that Prince
Edward, the King's son and heir apparent, had
always borne the same arms from the time of his
birth, with the difference of a silver label of
three points, to the said Prince of right belonging, and to no other subject whatever; that the
Earl of Surrey, unmindful of his allegiance, had,
as a false traitor and public enemy of the King,
conspired to withdraw his subjects from their
allegiance, and to deprive the King of his royal
dignity, on the 7th of October, 1546, in Kenninghall, in the county of Norfolk, in the house
of Thomas, Duke of Norfolk, his father, by
traitorously and openly causing the said arms of
the King, with three silver labels, to be painted
in conjunction with his own proper arms, thereby intending to repress, destroy, annihilate, and
scandalize the true and undoubted title of the
said Lord, the now King to the crown of this
his realm of England; and also traitorously to
disinherit and interrupt the said Lord Prince
Edward of his true and undoubted title in and
to the said crown of this realm of England, and
then and there maliciously, voluntarily, and
traitorously giving occasion whereby the said
Lord the now King might be disturbed and in-
terrupted in his said true title to the said crown
of this his realm of England, to the scandal,
peril, derogation, and contempt of the said Lord
the now King and of his said lawful title to his
said crown of England. [1]

[1] Dr. Nott, in his Memoir of the Earl, p. ci, has printed

In proof of this charge Mrs. Holland, the
Duke of Norfolk's mistress, deposed in general
terms that he had reproached Surrey for his
want of skill in quartering his arms.   The
Duchess of Richmond declared that he had
spoken with asperity of Hertford, to whom he
attributed his late imprisonment ; that he had
shown dislike to the new nobility; had complained that the King expressed displeasure for
the defeat at Boulogne in the preceding year ;
that he had dissuaded her from reading too far
in the scriptures ; and that he had erected an
altar in a church at Boulogne : but in the conclusion of her deposition, she maliciously in-
sinuated that the earl had surmounted his arms
instead of with a coronet, with what " seemed
to her much like a close crown, and a cipher
which she took to be the king's cipher, H.R."

a document found in the Heralds' College, of a conversation
between Surrey and the Richmond Herald respecting an
alteration in his arms, which took place whilst Surrey was
still in favour, and before he went to Boulogne.   This document was probably adduced against him upon his trial.
Charles Young (now Garter) discovered the original in the
library of the College of Arms.   It is in a collection of various papers, bound up together, and given by Sir William
Dugdale to the College.   He has also ascertained that Sir
Gilbert Dethycke was the Richmond Herald there alluded
to, and it also appears clear to him that Sir Chris. Barker,
then garter king at arms, was the person with whom the
conversation was held. He appeared as a witness at Surrey's
trial, and if the conversation stated be the summary of his
evidence, it would prove that he added great ingratitude to
his impatience, and the ignorance in his profession, which
he then made proof of. (*Memorials of the Howard Family*, ed.
1837, No. VII.)

Sir Edmund Knyvett and Thomas Pope also gave their testimony, but it contained nothing of the slightest importance.

The crime for which this young nobleman was thus arraigned has never been properly examined ; and, satisfied with its manifest absurdity, historians as well as the biographers of Surrey have omitted to point out upon what grounds that inference is justified.

The arms of King Edward the Confessor are presumed to have been a blue field charged with a gold cross flory at the ends, between five gold martlets, a kind of swallow without legs ; but as heraldry was then unknown, it is extremely doubtful if this or any other bearing was used by that monarch. Arms appear to have been used by the kings of England in the reign of Richard the First, who bore a red shield, charged with three gold lions, which have ever since been deemed to be the arms of England. As early as the time of Edward the First, and probably about a century before, the arms of three saints were always borne on banners in the English army, and on all state occasions, namely, those of St. George, the tutelar saint of this country; of St. Edmund, and of St. Edward the Confessor, but neither of those ensigns was deemed to be connected with the sovereignty of England. Richard the Second, however, being actuated by extraordinary veneration for St. Edward the Confessor, chose him for his patron saint, and impaled his arms with those of England and France; and, at the same time, he

granted the Confessor's arms to be borne per
pale with the paternal coats of two or three of
the most eminent noblemen of the day, each of
whom was descended from the blood royal.
One of the persons so distinguished was Thomas
Mowbray, Earl of Nottingham and Duke of
Norfolk, the right to whose arms and quarterings was indisputably inherited by the Earl of
Surrey, but the right to the coat of the Confessor
depends upon whether it was granted to Mowbray
for life only, or to him *and his heirs*, a point
which has not been ascertained. Conceiving
himself, however, entitled to it,[1] Surrey in mar-
shaling his arms included it with his other
numerous quarterings, and the injustice of con-
struing the act into a treasonable design is still
more apparent from other circumstances. Neither
Henry the Eighth nor any other monarch after
Richard the Second, ever used the arms of the
Confessor in conjunction with their own, and
the statement that Prince Edward then did so
with a label, is not supported by any other evi-

[1] The Duke of Norfolk stated in his petition to Queen
Mary, to have his own and Surrey's attainder reversed :—

"And forasmuch most gracious Sovereign Lady as the offence wherewith your said subject and supplicant was charged,
and whereof he was indicted, was for bearing of arms, which
he and his ancestors had heretofore of long time and continuance borne, as well within this realm as without, and as
well also in the presence of the said late King, as in the presence of divers of his noble progenitors, Kings of England,
and which said arms your said supplicant and subject, and
his ancestors might lawfully and justly bear and give, as by
good and substantial matter of record it may and doth appear."

dence. Surrey introduced the label as the proper distinction of his arms from those of his father, so that he appears to have done nothing that he was not authorized by law to do; and even at this moment heralds allow the Confessor's arms to several noble families. It is remarkable that whilst this preposterous accusation was brought against Surrey, he himself bore the *royal* arms by virtue of his descent from Thomas of Brotherton,[1] the son of Edward the First, whilst various other noblemen in the reign of Henry the Eighth quartered the royal arms of England and France, and two if not more of them, the Duke of Buckingham and the Earl of Wiltshire, had borne them, not in the inferior position of the third or fourth, but in the *first* quarter, as their paternal arms with impunity, and as a matter of acknowledged right.[2]

Surrey was brought to trial at the Guildhall on the 13th January, 1547, when he defended himself with singular courage and ability, by im-

[1] It is a singular fact, that when Henry the Eighth granted armorial ensigns to Anne Boleyn, then Marchioness of Pembroke, he took especial care to shew her *royal* and illustrious descent through *the Howards*, by introducing the arms of Thomas of Brotherton, son of Edward the First, and of the Warrens, Earls of Surrey, out of the *Howard* shield. In the arms of Katharine Howard, Henry impaled with his own the same royal quartering of Brotherton, whilst in farther evidence of her royal descent, one of the quarterings was formed of the arms of France and England.

[2] It was for some centuries the Law of Arms, that whenever a person was entitled to quarter the royal arms, they were to take precedence of all others by being placed in the first quarter.

peaching the evidence brought against him, and
urging his right, on the authority of the Heralds
and of precedent, to bear the obnoxious arms.
When a witness asserted that, in a conversation
with the Earl, he repeated some strong expression
which Surrey had used, together with his own
insolent reply, the prisoner made no other observation than by turning to the Jury and saying,
" I leave it to you to judge whether it were probable that this man should speak thus to the Earl
of Surrey and he not strike him."

But neither eloquence, nor spirit, nor even in-
nocence itself, was likely to avail a man accused
of treason in the reign of Henry the Eighth; and
the Jury, among whom it is melancholy to find
two near relations of his faithful attendant Clere,
found him guilty. He was remanded to the
Tower, and beheaded on the 21st of January,
just eight days after his conviction, and when he
was only thirty years of age.[1]

No particulars are preserved of his deportment
in prison or on the scaffold; but from the noble
spirit he evinced at his trial, and from his general
character, it cannot be doubted that he behaved
in the last scene of his existence with fortitude
and dignity. On the barbarous injustice to which

[1] For some particulars of the trial of the Earl of Surrey
consult Herbert's *Life and Reign of Henry VIII.*, fol. 1672,
p. 626; Burnet's *History of the Reformation*, i. 345; and
the " First Part of the Inventory and Calendar of the Con
tents of the Baga de Secretis," printed in the Third Report
of the Deputy Keeper of the Public Records, Feb. 28, 1842,
Appendix, p. 267.

he was sacrificed comment is unnecessary, but
regret at his early fate is increased by the circumstance that Henry himself, whose name is a
disgrace to any country, in any age, was in
extremities when he ordered his execution. His
swollen and enfeebled hands having been long
unequal to the task of guiding a pen, a stamp,
with the facsimile of the initials " H. R.," was
affixed to the death-warrant in his presence.[1] In
like manner was that for the execution of the
Duke of Norfolk signed ; but the King dying
within the same week, his life was preserved.
Surrey was buried in the church of All Hallows-
Barking, Tower Street, but his body was removed to Framlingham by his son, the Earl of
Northampton, where he erected a handsome
monument to his father's memory, with this
inscription :—

HENRICO . HOWARDO . THOMÆ . SECUNDI . DUCIS
NORFOLCIÆ . FILIO . PRIMOGENITO . THOMÆ . TERTII
PATRI . COMITI . SURRIÆ . ET . GEORGIANI . ORDINIS
EQUITI . AURATO . IMMATURE . ANNO . SALUTIS
MDXLVI . ABREPTO . ET . FRANCISCÆ . UXORI
EJUS. FILIÆ. JOHANNIS. COMITIS. OXONIÆ. HENRICUS
HOWARDUS . COMES . NORTHAMPTONIÆ . FILIUS
SECUNDO . GENITUS . HOC . SUPREMUM . PIETATIS
IN . PARENTES . MONUMENTUM . POSUIT
ANNO . DOMINI . MDCXIV.

[1] On August 31, 1546, Henry appointed A. Denny, J.
Gate, and William Clere, to sign all instruments requiring
his signature in the following manner : two   them were to
impress a dry stamp upon the instrument, and the third to
fill up the impression with pen and ink.

The monument of the Earl of Surrey at Framlingham is an elevated tomb, with his arms and those of his lady in the front, in the angles, and an inscription in the centre.   His effigy in armour, with an ermined mantle, his feet bearing against a lion couchant.   His lady, in black, with an ermined mantle and a coronet, on his left, and both having their hands joined in prayer. On a projecting plynth in front is the figure of his second son, the Earl of Northampton, in armour, with a mantle of ermine, kneeling in prayer.   Behind, on a similar plynth, kneeling, with a coronet and in robes, his eldest daughter, Jane, Countess of Westmoreland, on the right; and his third daughter, Catherine, the wife of Henry Lord Berkeley, kneeling on the left. The monument is kept in order, and painted occasionally, as directed by the will of the Earl of Northampton, out of the endowment of his hospital at Greenwich.   In making a repair of this monument in October, 1835, the Rev. George Attwood, curate of Framlingham, discovered the remains of the Earl lying imbedded in clay, directly under his figure on his tomb.

Whatever may have been the Earl's happiness in his own family, the situation of his parents must have occasioned him much uneasiness; and it is to be regretted that his mother should have had to accuse him of unkindness.   For several years after their marriage the Duke and Duchess lived together in comparative harmony; and it does not appear when the discord first commenced.   She bore him five children; and at a period long after the event, she charged him with great cruelty at the time of the birth of the Duchess of Richmond; but this he absolutely denied. The principal cause of alienation was the Duke's attachment to a lady whom the Duchess terms "that drab, Bess Holland," and which attachment was supposed by the Duchess to have commenced nearly seven years before her separation from him. It added to the Duchess's mortification that her daughter, the Duchess of Richmond, associated with this person. It was in 1534 that the final quarrel and separation took place; when the Duchess went to reside at Redborne in Hertfordshire, which she describes as a "hard" or expensive country. From not receiving a proper allowance for her support, she complained to Cromwell, the Lord Privy Seal, praying him to intercede on her behalf. Her letters, which are curious, are preserved in the Cottonian collection (Titus B. i.), and were consulted by Lord Herbert of Cherbury for his *History of the Reign of Henry VIII*, and are printed by Dr. Nott in the Appendix to his Life of the Earl of Surrey. The Duke of Norfolk died in 1554, and the Duchess survived him four years. She died on Nov. 30, 1558, and was buried in the Howard Chapel, Lambeth, where was formerly an epitaph written by her brother, Henry Lord Stafford.

Lord Surrey left two sons, Thomas, then about the age of eleven, who became the fourth Duke of Norfolk; and Henry, who was created, by James the First, Lord Howard of Marnhill and

e

Earl of Northampton; and three daughters: Jane, who married Charles Neville Earl of Westmoreland; Katharine, who became the wife of Henry Lord Berkeley; and Margaret, who married Henry Lord Scrope of Bolton. All which is known of his widow, the Countess Frances, is, that she married secondly, in the reign of Edward the Sixth, Thomas Steyning, of Woodford, in Suffolk, Esq., by whom she had a daughter, Mary, who married Charles Seckford, Esq. The Countess died at Soham Earl, about a mile and a half from Framlingham, on the 30th June, 1577, thirty years after the death of the Earl of Surrey.

A curious inventory of Surrey's apparel is particularly deserving of notice, from the manner in which it was distributed among his enemies the Seymours, and others, by the Crown, to which it fell by his attainder. These rapacious favourites considered nothing too trifling for their acceptance, and their conduct affords a humiliating idea of a nobleman of the sixteenth century. Both the Protector and his brother partook also very largely of the Duke of Norfolk's jewels and other property.

ALL THESE TO THE DUKE OF SOMERSET.—One Parliament robe of purple velvet, with a garter set upon the shoulder; four black velvet caps, set with pearl and goldsmiths' work; a hat of crimson satin and crimson velvet, with a white feather; a scarf of crimson gold, sarcenet; two pairs of knit hose; two dozen arming points; a knit petticoat; two rapiers, all gilt, graven antique; two daggers, all gilt and graven, appendant to two girdles; a gilt dagger, with a sheath of black velvet; a pair of stirrups, all gilt; ditto, parcel gilt; another pair of stirrups; two pair of spurs gilt; a horse harness of black velvet, set with studs, of copper, and gilt; a fod cloth of black velvet, fringed with Venice gold; a horse harness of crimson velvet, fringed with Venice gold.

To Mr. COLLEY AND Mr. THORP.—A robe, with hood, and crimson velvet.

To Mr. BRIAN.—A gown of cloth of gold, furred and faced with sables.

ALL THESE TO SIR HENRY SEYMOUR.—A gown of black velvet, with a curious guard of black satin; a gown of crimson taffeta, faced with busard: a coat and cassock of black velvet, the one wrought with satin, and the other with satin and wreaths; a cape of frizardo, guarded upon with velvet, and embroidered upon with russet satin; with other doublets, hoses, caps and shirts.

Mr. FOWLER.—A gown of black satin embroidered and lined with gold sarcenet; a cassock of black silk embroidered and lined with gold sarcenet.

Mrs. WINFRED FISHER.—A robe of black velvet set with buttons of gold enamelled black and white; a pair of hose, black velvet, laid on with threads of Venice gold.

Mr. PHILPOT.—A robe of black velvet, embroidered with tawney satin; with other doublets and hoses.

Mr. T. ALLEN.—A doublet of black satin cut.

Mr. COLLEY AND Mr. THORP.—A shirt wrought with black silk to each.

It is difficult to pronounce a certain opinion upon Surrey's personal character. Dr. Nott and his other biographers have spoken of his merits in a strain of eulogy which, to say the least, is not borne out by the few notices that are preserved of him. That he was accomplished is amply manifested by his works, which also indicate a correct moral taste, since there is not, in the whole of his poems, one word, or an allusion to a single thought, to which the most fastidious person can possibly object. This merit deserves greater praise than it has hitherto re-

ceived, because he is almost the first English
versifier who possessed it ; and it is no slight
proof of the purity of his mind. Surrey's greatest
fault appears to have been a naturally hasty and
impetuous temper, which, in a man of exalted
rank and great influence, was probably increased by his station exacting deference and
submission from the greater part of those with
whom he came in contact. In his brief career
he was imprisoned no less than three times, and
ultimately lost his life from his imprudent conduct ; and the only excuse which can be made
for him is, that he was young, and that he was
too proud and too ingenuous to conceal what
he thought. His conduct towards the Duchess
of Norfolk has been already adverted to, and
whatever may have been her errors, the son who
could, under any circumstances, treat his mother
with unkindness has slight claim to be considered
an amiable man. Surrey's military talents and his
ardent courage do not admit of being questioned,
and his veneration for his father tends, in a slight
degree, to redeem his behaviour towards his
mother. Examples of his zeal for his friends,
and of his deep sense of honour, have been adduced in this memoir, and they certainly entitle
his memory to respect, whilst his conduct as a
husband and a father has never been impeached.

Of the writings of Surrey, and the rank to
which he is entitled among the poets of England,
the remarks of Puttenham, Warton, Henry,
Dr. Nott, Hallam, and D'Israeli, contain all
which can be said on the subject. Pope brought

him into notice during the last century by the following pasage in the *Windsor Forest,* which occasioned his poems to be immediately reprinted twice :—

> " Here noble Surrey felt the sacred rage,
> Surrey, the Granville of a former age;
> Matchless his pen, victorious was his lance;
> Bold in the lists, and graceful in the dance :
> In the same shades the Cupids tun'd his lyre,
> To the same notes of love and soft desire;
> Fair Geraldine, bright object of his vow,
> Then fill'd the groves, as heavenly Myra now."

It is difficult to give extracts from Dr. Nott's remarks on Surrey's writings, but the following passages seem to convey all that is material :—

" Surrey perceived that some change in our versification was unavoidable, and he attempted a change, which was conceived, as the event has proved, in a perfect knowledge of the nature and genius of the English language. The change he proposed and effected was this. He substituted for the old rhythmical mode of versification one, as nearly metrical as the nature of any language, which regulates the value of syllables by accent, and not by quantity, will allow. He limited the heroic verse to ten syllables, and these he divided into five equal Iambic feet; for he perceived that the frequent return of the short syllable was necessary to correct that languor and ponderosity which the constant recurrence of monosyllables would otherwise occasion. He was aware, however, that the Iambic measure, though sweet in itself, was liable to become

monotonous and pall upon the ear. He therefore introduced the further refinement of breaking the lines with pauses. The natural place
for the pause was at the end of the fourth syllable
where the old cæsura generally fell; but he
varied the situation of his pauses as he found
the harmony of the verse required, or as he
thought the beauty and effect of the passage
would be heightened by it.

"Such was the system of versification introduced by Surrey. Of the correctness of his
taste and the justness of his reasoning upon the
subject, no further proof need be required than
the event. For the laws of English versification, such as they were established by Surrey,
have been adopted by our standard writers,
with hardly any variation, ever since. At particular times, indeed, a particular taste has for
a short season prevailed. Thus in the reign of
James, and of Charles the First, quaintness,
and a love of antithesis gave a new turn to our
versification, and made it abrupt and irregular.
But in the two best epochs of our poetry, during
the reign of Elizabeth and after the Restoration,
those principles of versification alone were observed which Surrey had introduced. An at-
tentive reader will be surprised to find how
little was added afterwards by even Dryden or
Pope to the system and perfectness of Surrey's
numbers.

"Surrey first rejected the use of those 'au-
reate and mellifluate' terms, which he found
disfiguring our language with a sort of pre-

scriptive tyranny, and restricted himself to the use of those words alone which were approved by common use, and were natural to the language.

." He next introduced a studied mode of involution in his periods, which gives dignity to what is so expressed, and a certain remoteness from common life, essential to the higher branches of poetic composition. And lastly, he discountenanced altogether the French mode of laying an unnatural stress upon final syllables; he followed the obvious and common pronunciation of our language; carefully avoiding all double terminations, and using only those words for rhyme which were noble and harmonious, and such as the ear might dwell upon with pleasure.

" Such were the improvements made by Surrey in our versification and poetic diction. These alone, had nothing more been effected by him, would have entitled him to the praise of having been the restorer of modern English poetry. But we owe to him further obligations. He first introduced the use of Blank Heroic Verse. In this respect the praise is exclusively his own. In reforming our versification and poetic diction, he had in some degree Chaucer for his guide; and in some degree he was conducted by the bent and genius of our language. When he attempted blank verse he had no guide whatever, as far as we have yet been able to discover, but his own judgment and taste. All writers are agreed that Surrey's trans-

lation of the Second and Fourth Book of
Virgil's Æneid is the first specimen of Heroic
Blank Verse in our language.

" The leading features of Surrey's style were
chiefly dignity and compression. Of his compression, contrasted with the diffusive mode of
writing used by all the authors who preceded
him, a more striking instance cannot well be
found than that which occurs in the opening to
his sonnet on Sir Thomas Wyatt's death.

" The reader's observation will enable him
easily to collect from Surrey's poems other instances of elegant and nervous compression. I
do not recollect a single passage where a thought
is needlessly expanded for the sake of filling up
a line. Surrey's style bears a stronger resem-
blance to Dryden's than to that of any other of
our poets. The same manliness, and ease, and
vigour characterizes both. In neither do we
find any affection of prettiness ; they seem both
to have been more intent on their thoughts than
their words ; they gave their words, indeed, a
full and a due consideration, but, as always ought
to be the case, in subserviency to their thoughts.

" It now remains to shew, that I have not
laboured to give a higher importance to Surrey's
writings, than they in reality possess. But how
shall we appreciate his writings too highly, who
by a single effort of genius corrected a nation's
taste, and shewed them first the way to that per-
fection in poetry, to which they have since attained? That the great change which in the
sixteenth century took place in our national poetry,

was owing chiefly to the influence of Surrey's writings, seems to me incontestable from the general popularity which they obtained immediately upon their appearance : and the studied imitation of them to be traced in all our poets in succession, from Sackville down to Spenser.

" Of the popularity of Surrey's poems, we have a convincing proof in the rapidity with which editions were multiplied. They were first printed in June, 1557. In the course of that and the following month they went through no less than four distinct impressions. [1] They were afterwards reprinted in 1565, in 1567 and in 1569, twice afterwards in 1574, again in 1585, and again in 1587. Besides this, selections from Surrey's poems were printed almost daily, with other popular pieces in single sheets, and in small collections called garlands ; by means of which they were made familiar to readers of the lower orders : whilst some of them, as we learn from the books of the Stationers' Company, were moralized ; a circumstance which of itself is sufficient to prove their popularity, and extensive circulation. [2] In addition to these facts we are to consider yet further, that Surrey's verses continued to be multiplied in manuscript by many

[1] Mr. Collier says, " There may possibly have been three impressions in 1557; but we are convinced that there were not four." (*Bibliographical Account of Early English Literature*, ii. 403.)

[2] " Surrey's pleasing little ode, ' When raging love with extreme pain,' which seems to have been a very popular piece, was printed in 1568 by J. Alde, moralized into ' When raging lust,' &c. ' Give place, ye ladies,' &c : was often reprinted as a ballad."

who had not the means of purchasing printed
copies ; and that they uniformly made part of
all the printed miscellanies of those days, up to
the beginning of the seventeenth century.   It
would be difficult to find an instance of any
poet in any country whose works were in so
short a time more widely circulated.   And if
so, we might ask, whether it would be possible
that writings thus largely diffused, and thus
universally admired, should not produce a
general and a lasting effect on public taste."

THE PRINTER TO THE READER. [1]

HAT to have well written in verse, yea, and in small parcels, deserveth great praise, the works of divers Latins, Italians, and others, do prove sufficiently. That our tongue is able in that kind to do as praiseworthily as the rest, the honourable style of the noble Earl of Surrey, and the weightiness of the deep witted Sir Thomas Wyatt the elder's verse, with several graces in sundry good English writers do show abundantly. It resteth now, gentle reader, that thou think it not evil done, to publish, to the honour of the English tongue, and for profit of the studious of English eloquence, those works which the ungentle horders up of such treasure have heretofore envied thee. And for this point, good reader, thine own profit and pleasure, in these presently, and in more hereafter, shall answer for my defence. If, perhaps, some mislike the stateliness of style removed from the rude skill of common ears, I ask help of the learned to

[1] This address by Tottel appeared in the first impression of 1557.

defend their learned friends, the authors of this work. And I exhort the unlearned, by reading to learn to be more skilful, and to purge that swine-like grossness, that maketh the sweet marjoram not to smell to their delight.

SONGS AND SONNETS.

DESCRIPTION OF THE RESTLESS STATE

OF A LOVER,

WITH SUIT TO HIS LADY, TO RUE ON HIS

DYING HEART.

THE sun hath twice brought forth his
    tender green,
Twice clad the earth in lively lusti-
    ness;
Once have the winds the trees de-
    spoiled clean,
And once again begins their cruelness;
Since I have hid under my breast the harm
That never shall recover healthfulness.
The winter's hurt recovers with the warm;
The parched green restored is with shade;
What warmth, alas! may serve for to disarm
The frozen heart, that mine in flame hath made?

B

What cold again is able to restore
My fresh green years, that wither thus and fade?
Alas! I see nothing hath hurt so sore
But Time, in time, reduceth a return:
In time my harm increaseth more and more,
And seems to have my cure always in scorn.
Strange kinds of death, in life that I do try!
At hand, to melt; far off, in flame to burn.
And like as time list to my cure apply,
So doth each place my comfort clean refuse.
All thing alive, that seeth the heavens with eye,
With cloak of night may cover, and excuse
Itself from travail of the day's unrest,
Save I, alas! against all others use,
That then stir up the torments of my breast;
And curse each star as causer of my fate.
And when the sun hath eke the dark opprest,
And brought the day, it doth nothing abate
The travails of mine endless smart and pain.
For then, as one that hath the light in hate,
I wish for night, more covertly to plain,
And me withdraw from every haunted place,
Lest by my chere[1] my chance appear to plain.
And in my mind I measure pace by pace,
To seek the place where I myself had lost,
That day that I was tangled in the lace,
In seeming slack that knitteth ever most:
But never yet the travail of my thought,
Of better state, could catch a cause to boast.
For if I found, sometime that I have sought,
Those stars by whom I trusted of the port,
My sails do fall, and I advance right nought;

[1] Behaviour, looks.

As anchor'd fast, my spirits do all resort
To stand agazed, and sink in more and more[1]
The deadly harm which she doth take in sport.
Lo! if I seek, how I do find my sore!
And if I flee, I carry with me still
The venom'd shaft, which doth his force restore
By haste of flight; and I may plain my fill
Unto myself, unless this careful song
Print in your heart some parcel of my tene.[2]
For I, alas! in silence all too long,
Of mine old hurt yet feel the wound but green.
Rue on my life; or else your cruel wrong
Shall well appear, and by my death be seen.

DESCRIPTION OF SPRING,

WHEREIN EACH THING RENEWS, SAVE ONLY

THE LOVER.

HE soote[3] season, that bud and bloom
forth brings,
With green hath clad the hill, and
eke the vale:
The nightingale with feathers new she sings;
The turtle to her make[4] hath told her tale;
Summer is come, for every spray now springs,
The hart hath hung his old head on the pale;

---

[1] To stand *at gaze* and *suck* in more and more. MSS.
cited by Dr. Nott.

[2] i.e. Sorrow.   [3] Sweet.   [4] Mate.

The buck in brake his winter coat he flings;
The fishes flete with new repaired scale;
The adder all her slough away she slings;
The swift swallow pursueth the flies smale;[1]
The busy bee her honey now she mings;[2]
Winter is worn that was the flowers' bale.[3]
    And thus I see among these pleasant things
    Each care decays, and yet my sorrow springs!

DESCRIPTION OF THE RESTLESS STATE
OF A LOVER.

W HEN youth had led me half the race
    That Cupid's scourge had made me run;
I looked back to mete the place
From whence my weary course begun.

And then I saw how my desire,
Misguiding me, had led the way:
Mine eyen, too greedy of their hire,
Had made me lose a better prey.

For when in sighs I spent the day,
And could not cloak my grief with game;
The boiling smoke did still bewray
The persaunt[4] heat of secret flame.

[1] Small.   [2] Mingles.
[3] Destruction.   [4] Or, present.

And when salt tears do bain my breast,
Where Love his pleasant trains hath sown ;
Her beauty hath the fruits opprest,
Ere that the buds were sprong and blown.

And when mine eyen did still pursue
The flying chase of their request ;
Their greedy looks did oft renew
The hidden wound within my breast.

When every look these cheeks might stain,
From deadly pale to glowing red ;
By outward signs appeared plain,
The woe wherein my heart was fed.[1]

But all too late Love learneth me
To paint all kind of colours new ;
To blind their eyes that else should see
My speckled cheeks with Cupid's hue.

And now the covert breast I claim,
That worshipp'd Cupid secretly ;
And nourished his sacred flame,
From whence no blazing sparks do fly.

[1] Some editions read :—
        " To her for help my heart was fled."

DESCRIPTION OF THE FICKLE AFFEC-
TIONS, PANGS, AND SLIGHTS
OF LOVE.

UCH wayward ways hath Love, that most
part in discord
Our wills do stand, whereby our hearts
but seldom do accord.
Deceit is his delight, and to beguile and mock
The simple hearts, whom he doth strike with fro-
ward, diverse stroke.
He causeth the one to rage with golden burning
dart ;
And doth allay with leaden cold again the other's
heart.
Hot gleams of burning fire, and easy sparks of
flame,
In balance of unequal weight he pondereth by aim.
From easy ford, where I might wade and pass full
well,
He me withdraws, and doth me drive into a deep
dark hell ;
And me withholds where I am call'd and offer'd
place,
And wills me that my mortal foe I do beseech of
grace ;
He lets me to pursue a conquest well near won,
To follow where my pains were lost, ere that my
suit begun.

So by this means I know how soon a heart may
    turn
From war to peace, from truce to strife, and so
    again return.
I know how to content myself in others lust;
Of little stuff unto myself to weave a web of trust;
And how to hide my harms with soft dissembling
    chere,
When in my face the painted thoughts would out-
    wardly appear.
I know how that the blood forsakes the face for
    dread;
And how by shame it stains again the cheeks with
    flaming red.
I know under the green, the serpent how he lurks;
The hammer of the restless forge I wot eke how it
    works.
I know, and can by rote the tale that I would tell;
But oft the words come forth awry of him that
    loveth well.
I know in heat and cold the lover how he shakes;
In singing how he doth complain; in sleeping how
    he wakes.
To languish without ache, sickless for to consume,
A thousand things for to devise, resolving all in
    fume.
And though he list to see his lady's grace full sore;
Such pleasures as delight his eye, do not his health
    restore.
I know to seek the track of my desired foe,
And fear to find that I do seek.   But chiefly this
    I know,
That lovers must transform into the thing beloved,

And live, (alas! who could believe?) with sprite
    from life removed.
I know in hearty sighs, and laughters of the spleen,
At once to change my state, my will, and eke my
    colour clean.
I know how to deceive myself with others help;
And how the lion chastised is, by beating of the
    whelp.
In standing near my fire, I know how that I freeze;
Far off I burn; in both I waste, and so my life I
    lese.
I know how love doth rage upon a yielding mind;
How small a net may take, and meash a heart of
    gentle kind:
Or else with seldom sweet to season heaps of gall;
Revived with a glimpse of grace, old sorrows to
    let fall.
The hidden trains I know, and secret snares of love;
How soon a look will print a thought, that never
    may remove.
The slipper state I know, the sudden turns from
    wealth,
The doubtful hope, the certain woe, and sure des-
    pair of health.

COMPLAINT OF A LOVER THAT DEFIED

LOVE,

AND WAS BY LOVE AFTER THE MORE TORMENTED.

WHEN summer took in hand the winter
  to assail,
  With force of might, and virtue great,
   his stormy blasts to quail:
And when he clothed fair the earth about with
  green,
And every tree new garmented, that pleasure was
  to seen:
Mine heart gan new revive, and changed blood
  did stir,
Me to withdraw my winter woes, that kept within
  the dore.[1]
' Abroad,' quoth my desire, ' assay to set thy foot;
Where thou shalt find the savour sweet; for
  sprong is every root.
And to thy health, if thou were sick in any case,
Nothing more good than in the spring the air to
  feel a space.
There shalt thou hear and see all kinds of birds
  y-wrought,
Well tune their voice with warble small, as nature
  hath them taught.'
Thus pricked me my lust the sluggish house to
  leave,

---

[1] Door.

And for my health I thought it best such counsel
    to receive.
So on a morrow forth, unwist of any wight,
I went to prove how well it would my heavy bur-
    den light.
And when I felt the air so pleasant round about,
Lord! to myself how glad I was that I had gotten
    out.
There might I see how Ver[1] had every blossom
    hent,[2]
And eke the new betrothed birds, y-coupled how
    they went;
And in their songs, methought, they thanked
    Nature much,
That by her license all that year to love, their hap
    was such,
Right as they could devise to choose them feres[3]
    throughout:
With much rejoicing to their Lord, thus flew they
    all about.
Which when I gan resolve, and in my head con-
    ceive,
What pleasant life, what heaps of joy, these little
    birds receive;
And saw in what estate I, weary man, was wrought,
By want of that, they had at will, and I reject at
    nought;
Lord! how I gan in wrath unwisely me demean!
I cursed Love, and him defied; I thought to turn
    the stream.

[1] Spring.
[2] Taken hold of, i.e. brought out every blossom.
[3] Companions, mates.

But when I well beheld, he had me under awe,
I asked mercy for my fault, that so transgrest his
    law!
' Thou blinded god,' quoth I, ' forgive me this
    offence,
Unwittingly I went about, to malice thy pretence.'
Wherewith he gave a beck, and thus methought
    he swore:
' Thy sorrow ought suffice to purge thy fault, if it
    were more.'
The virtue of which sound mine heart did so
    revive,
That I, methought, was made as whole as any man
    alive.
But here I may perceive mine error, all and some,
For that I thought that so it was; yet was it still
    undone ;
And all that was no more but mine impressed mind,
That fain would have some good relief, of Cupid
    well assign'd.
I turned home forthwith, and might perceive it well,
That he aggrieved was right sore with me for my
    rebel.
My harms have ever since increased more and
    more,
And I remain, without his help, undone for ever-
    more.
A mirror let me be unto ye lovers all;
Strive not with Love; for if ye do, it will ye thus
    befall.

COMPLAINT OF A LOVER REBUKED.[1]

LOVE, that liveth and reigneth in my
  thought,
 That built his seat within my captive
  breast;
Clad in the arms wherein with me he fought,
Oft in my face he doth his banner rest.
She, that me taught to love, and suffer pain;
My doubtful hope, and eke my hot desire
With shamefast cloak to shadow and restrain,
Her smiling grace converteth straight to ire.
And coward Love then to the heart apace
Taketh his flight; whereas he lurks, and plains
His purpose lost, and dare not shew his face.
For my Lord's guilt thus faultless bide I pains.
 Yet from my Lord shall not my foot remove:
 Sweet is his death, that takes his end by love.

COMPLAINT OF THE LOVER DISDAINED.

IN Cyprus springs, whereas dame Venus
  dwelt,
 A well so hot, that whoso tastes the
  same,
Were he of stone, as thawed ice should melt,

---

[1] Translated from Petrarch, part i, sonnet 109. Wyatt
also translated it: see his Poems, p. 1.

And kindled find his breast with fired flame;
Whose moist poison dissolved hath my hate.
This creeping fire my cold limbs so opprest,
That in the heart that harbour'd freedom late,
Endless despair long thraldom hath imprest.
Another so cold in frozen ice is found,[1]
Whose chilling venom of repugnant kind,
The fervent heat doth quench of Cupid's wound,
And with the spot of change infects the mind;
   Whereof my dear hath tasted to my pain:
   My service thus is grown into disdain.[2]

DESCRIPTION AND PRAISE OF HIS LOVE

GERALDINE.

FROM Tuscane came my Lady's worthy
      race;
   Fair Florence was sometime her[3] an-
     cient seat:
The western isle, whose pleasant shore doth face
Wild Camber's cliffs, did give her lively heat:
Foster'd she was with milk of Irish breast:
Her sire an Earl; her dame of Princes blood.
From tender years, in Britain she doth rest,
With Kinges child; where she tasteth costly[4] food.

[1] Another well of frozen ice is found.—*Nott.*
[2] Whereby my service grows into disdain.—*Nott.*
[3] i. e. Their.
[4] Ghostly, in some printed copies.

Hunsdon did first present her to mine eyen :
Bright is her hue, and Geraldine she hight.
Hampton me taught to wish her first for mine ;
And Windsor, alas ! doth chase me from her sight.
 Her beauty of kind ; her virtues from above ;
 Happy is he that can obtain her love !

THE FRAILTY AND HURTFULNESS OF

BEAUTY.[1]

RITTLE beauty, that Nature made so
   frail,
  Whereof the gift is small, and short
   the season ;
Flowering to-day, to-morrow apt to fail ;
Tickle treasure, abhorred of reason :
Dangerous to deal with, vain, of none avail ;
Costly in keeping, past not worth two peason ;[2]
Slipper in sliding, as is an eel's tail ;
Hard to attain, once gotten, not geason :[3]
Jewel of jeopardy, that peril doth assail ;
False and untrue, enticed oft to treason ;
Enemy to youth, that most may I bewail ;
Ah ! bitter sweet, infecting as the poison,
 Thou farest as fruit that with the frost is taken ;
 To day ready ripe, to-morrow all to shaken.

[1] In the Harrington MS. this poem is attributed to Lord
Vaux.
 [2] Two pease.   [3] Rare, or uncommon.

A COMPLAINT BY NIGHT OF THE LOVER
NOT BELOVED.

LAS! so all things now do hold their
    peace!
Heaven and earth disturbed in nothing;
The beasts, the air, the birds their song
    do cease,
The nightès car [1] the stars about doth bring.
Calm is the sea; the waves work less and less:
So am not I, whom love, alas! doth wring,
Bringing before my face the great increase
Of my desires, whereat I weep and sing,
In joy and woe, as in a doubtful case.
For my sweet thoughts sometime do pleasure bring;
But by and by, the cause of my disease
Gives me a pang, that inwardly doth sting,
    When that I think what grief it is again,
    To live and lack the thing should rid my pain.

HOW EACH THING, SAVE THE LOVER IN

SPRING, REVIVETH TO PLEASURE.

HEN Windsor walls sustain'd my
    wearied arm;
My hand my chin, to ease my rest-
    less head;
The pleasant plot revested green with warm;

[1] Chare.

The blossom'd boughs, with lusty Ver[1] y-spread;
The flower'd meads, the wedded birds so late
Mine eyes discover: and to my mind resort
The jolly woes, the hateless, short debate,
The rakehell[2] life, that 'longs to love's disport.
Wherewith, alas ! the heavy charge of care
Heap'd in my breast breaks forth, against my will,
In smoky sighs, that overcast the air.
My vapour'd eyes such dreary tears distil,
    The tender spring which quicken where they fall;
    And I half bent to throw me down withal.

A VOW TO LOVE FAITHFULLY, HOWSO-
EVER HE BE REWARDED.[3]

SET me whereas the sun doth parch the
        green,
     Or where his beams do not dissolve the
        ice;
In temperate heat, where he is felt and seen ;
In presence prest[4] of people, mad, or wise ;
Set me in high, or yet in low degree ;
In longest night, or in the shortest day ;
In clearest sky, or where clouds thickest be ;
In lusty youth, or when my hairs are gray : ·
Set me in heaven, in earth, or else in hell,

[1] Spring.   [2] Dissolute.
[3] Cf. Petrarch, Parte Prima, Son. 113; and Horace, Lib.
i. Ode 22.
[4] Query, press, i. e. in the presence of a crowd of people.

In hill, or dale, or in the foaming flood;
Thrall,[1] or at large, alive whereso I dwell,
Sick, or in health, in evil fame or good,
    Her's will I be; and only with this thought
    Content myself, although my chance be nought.

COMPLAINT THAT HIS LADY,

AFTER SHE KNEW HIS LOVE, KEPT HER FACE ALWAYS HIDDEN FROM HIM.

 NEVER saw my Lady lay apart
Her cornet[2] black, in cold nor yet in
    heat,
Sith first she knew my grief was grown
    so great;
Which other fancies driveth from my heart,
That to myself I do the thought reserve,
The which unwares did wound my woful breast;
But on her face mine eyes might never rest;
Yet, since she knew I did her love and serve,
Her golden tresses clad alway with black,
Her smiling looks that hid thus evermore,
And that restrains which I desire so sore.
So doth this cornet govern me, alack!
    In summer, sun, in winter's breath, a frost;
    Whereby the light of her fair looks I lost.

[1] In bondage.
[2] A head dress, with a hood or veil attached to it.

c

REQUEST TO HIS LOVE TO JOIN BOUNTY
WITH BEAUTY.

THE golden gift that Nature did thee
          give,
    To fasten friends, and feed them at thy
          will,
With form and favour, taught me to believe,
How thou art made to shew her greatest skill.
Whose hidden virtues are not so unknown,
But lively domes [1] might gather at the first
Where beauty so her perfect seed hath sown,
Of other graces follow needs there must.
Now certes, Garret,[2] since all this is true,
That from above thy gifts are thus elect,
Do not deface them then with fancies new;
Nor change of minds, let not thy mind infect:
But mercy him thy friend that doth thee serve,
Who seeks alway thine honour to preserve.

[1] Judgments, or opinions.

[2] Dr. Nott observes, " The first quarto and all the other
editions, except the second and third quartos, read ' Now
certes, Lady.' Why the genuine reading given in the text
should have ever been suppressed it is difficult to say. The
Fitz-Gerald family almost always wrote their name Garret.
The Fair Geraldine, when attending on the Princess Mary,
was always called Garret: and she herself in her Will desig-
nates her sister, the Lady Margaret Fitz-Gerald, ' The
Lady Margaret Garret.' "

PRISONED IN WINDSOR, HE RECOUNTETH
HIS PLEASURE THERE PASSED.

O cruel prison how could betide, alas,
    As proud Windsor? where I, in lust
        and joy,
    With a King's son, my childish years
        did pass,
In greater feast than Priam's sons of Troy.
Where each sweet place returns a taste full sour.
The large green courts, where we were wont to
    hove,[1]
With eyes cast up into the Maiden's tower,
And easy sighs, such as folk draw in love.
The stately seats, the ladies bright of hue.
The dances short, long tales of great delight ;
With words and looks that tigers could but rue ;
Where each of us did plead the other's right.
The palme-play,[2] where, despoiled for the game,
With dazzled eyes oft we by gleams of love
Have miss'd the ball, and got sight of our dame,
To bait her eyes, which kept the leads above.
The gravel'd ground, with sleeves tied on the helm,
On foaming horse, with swords and friendly hearts;
With chere, as though one should another whelm,
Where we have fought, and chased oft with darts.
With silver drops the mead yet spread for ruth,
In active games of nimbleness and strength,
Where we did strain, trained with swarms of youth,
Our tender limbs, that yet shot up in length.

---

[1] Hover.   [2] Tennis-court.

The secret groves, which oft we made resound
Of pleasant plaint, and of our ladies' praise ;
Recording oft what grace each one had found,
What hope of speed, what dread of long delays.
The wild forest, the clothed holts with green ;
With reins availed, and swift y-breathed horse,
With cry of hounds, and merry blasts between,
Where we did chase the fearful hart of force.
The wide vales [1] eke, that harbour'd us each night :
Wherewith, alas ! reviveth in my breast
The sweet accord : such sleeps as yet delight :
The pleasant dreams, the quiet bed of rest ;
The secret thoughts, imparted with such trust ;
The wanton talk, the divers change of play ;
The friendship sworn, each promise kept so just,
Wherewith we past the winter night away.
And with this thought the blood forsakes the face ;
The tears berain [2] my cheeks of deadly hue :
The which, as soon as sobbing sighs, alas !
Up-supped have, thus I my plaint renew :
' O place of bliss ! renewer of my woes !
Give me account, where is my noble fere ? [3]
Whom in thy walls thou dost each night enclose ;
To other lief ; [4] but unto me most dear.'
Echo, alas ! that doth my sorrow rue,
Returns thereto a hollow sound of plaint.
Thus I alone, where all my freedom grew,
In prison pine, with bondage and restraint :
And with remembrance of the greater grief,
To banish the less, I find my chief relief.

[1] According to Dr. Nott, this line in the Harrington MS.
reads thus,

  The *void walls* eke, that harbour'd us each night.

[2] Bedew, as with rain.　　[3] Companion.　　[4] Endeared.

THE LOVER COMFORTETH HIMSELF WITH

THE WORTHINESS OF HIS LOVE.

HEN raging love with extreme pain
Most cruelly distrains my heart;
When that my tears, as floods of rain,
Bear witness of my woful smart;
When sighs have wasted so my breath
That I lie at the point of death:

I call to mind the navy great
That the Greeks brought to Troyè town:
And how the boisterous winds did beat
Their ships, and rent their sails adown;
Till Agamemnon's daughter's blood
Appeas'd the gods that them withstood.

And how that in those ten years war
Full many a bloody deed was done;
And many a lord that came full far,
There caught his bane, alas! too soon;
And many a good knight overrun,
Before the Greeks had Helen won.

Then think I thus: ' Sith such repair,
So long time war of valiant men,
Was all to win a lady fair,
Shall I not learn to suffer then?

And think my life well spent to be,
Serving a worthier wight than she?'

Therefore I never will repent,
But pains contented still endure;
For like as when, rough winter spent,
The pleasant spring straight draweth in ure;[1]
So after raging storms of care,
Joyful at length may be my fare.

COMPLAINT OF THE ABSENCE OF HER

LOVER BEING UPON THE SEA.

 HAPPY dames! that may embrace
The fruit of your delight;
Help to bewail the woful case,
And eke the heavy plight
Of me, that wonted to rejoice
The fortune of my pleasant choice:
Good ladies! help to fill my mourning voice.

In ship, freight with remembrance
Of thoughts and pleasures past,
He sails that hath in governance
My life, while it will last;
With scalding sighs, for lack of gale,
Furthering his hope, that is his sail,
Toward me, the sweet port of his avail.

[1] In use.

Alas! how oft in dreams I see
Those eyes that were my food ;
Which sometime so delighted me,
That yet they do me good :
Wherewith I wake with his return,
Whose absent flame did make me burn :
But when I find the lack, Lord! how I mourn.

When other lovers in arms across,
Rejoice their chief delight ;
Drowned in tears, to mourn my loss,
I stand the bitter night
In my window, where I may see
Before the winds how the clouds flee :
Lo! what mariner love hath made me.

And in green waves, when the salt flood
Doth rise by rage of wind ;
A thousand fancies in that mood
Assail my restless mind.
Alas! now drencheth[1] my sweet foe,
That with the spoil of my heart did go,
And left me ; but, alas! why did he so ?

And when the seas wax calm again,
To chase from me annoy,
My doubtful hope doth cause me plain ;
So dread cuts off my joy.
Thus is my wealth mingled with woe,
And of each thought a doubt doth grow ;
Now he comes! will he come? alas! no, no!

[1] Is drowned.

COMPLAINT OF A DYING LOVER

REFUSED UPON HIS LADY'S UNJUST MISTAKING OF

HIS WRITING.

N winter's just return, when Boreas gan
    his reign,
        And every tree unclothed fast, as na-
        ture taught them plain :
In misty morning dark, as sheep are then in hold,
I hied me fast, it sat me on, my sheep for to unfold.
And as it is a thing that lovers have by fits,
Under a palm I heard one cry as he had lost his
    wits.
Whose voice did ring so shrill in uttering of his
    plaint,
That I amazed was to hear how love could him
    attaint.
' Ah ! wretched man,' quoth he ; 'come, death,
    and rid this woe ;
A just reward, a happy end, if it may chance thee
    so.
Thy pleasures past have wrought thy woe without
    redress ;
If thou hadst never felt no joy, thy smart had been
    the less.'
And rechless of his life, he gan both sigh and groan :
A rueful thing me thought it was, to hear him
    make such moan.

' Thou cursed pen, said he, ' woe-worth the bird
    thee bare ;
The man, the knife, and all that made thee, woe
    be to their share :
Woe-worth the time and place where I so could
    indite ;
And woe be it yet once again, the pen that so can
    write.
Unhappy hand ! it had been happy time for me,
If when to write thou learned first, unjointed
    hadst thou be.'
Thus cursed he himself, and every other wight,
Save her alone whom love him bound to serve
    both day and night.
Which when I heard, and saw how he himself
    for-did ;[1]
Against the ground with bloody strokes, himself
    e'en there to rid ;
Had been my heart of flint, it must have melted
    tho' ;
For in my life I never saw a man so full of woe.
With tears, for his redress, I rashly to him ran,
And in my arms I caught him fast, and thus I
    spake him than :
' What woful wight art thou, that in such heavy
    case
Torments thyself with such despite, here in this
    desart place ?'
Wherewith, as all aghast, fulfill'd with ire and
    dread,
He cast on me a staring look, with colour pale and
    dead :

[1] Destroy.

' Nay, what art thou,' quoth he, 'that in this heavy
      plight
Dost find me here, most woful wretch, that life
      hath in despite ?'
' I am,' quoth I, ' but poor, and simple in degree;
A shepherd's charge I have in hand, unworthy
      though I be.'
With that he gave a sigh, as though the sky should
      fall,
And loud, alas! he shrieked oft, and, ' Shepherd,'
      gan he call,
' Come, hie thee fast at once, and print it in thy
      heart,
So thou shalt know, and I shall tell thee, guiltless
      how I smart.'
His back against the tree sore feebled all with faint,
With weary sprite he stretcht him up, and thus he
      told his plaint :
' Once in my heart,' quoth he, ' it chanced me to
      love
Such one, in whom hath Nature wrought, her
      cunning for to prove.
And sure I cannot say, but many years were spent,
With such good will so recompens'd, as both we
      were content.
Whereto then I me bound, and she likewise also,
The sun should run his course awry, ere we this
      faith forego.
Who joyed then but I ? who had this worldès bliss ?
Who might compare a life to mine, that never
      thought on this ?
But dwelling in this truth, amid my greatest joy,
Is me befallen a greater loss than Priam had of Troy.

She is reversed clean, and beareth me in hand,
That my deserts have given cause to break this
      faithful band:
And for my just excuse availeth no defence.
Now knowest thou all; I can no more; but, Shep-
      herd, hie thee hence,
And give him leave to die, that may no longer live:
Whose record, lo! I claim to have, my death I do
      forgive.
And eke when I am gone, be bold to speak it plain,
Thou hast seen die the truest man that ever love
      did pain.'
Wherewith he turned him round, and gasping oft
      for breath,
Into his arms a tree he raught, and said: 'Wel-
      come my death!
Welcome a thousand fold, now dearer unto me
Than should, without her love to live, an emperor
      to be.'
Thus in this woful state he yielded up the ghost;
And little knoweth his lady, what a lover she hath
      lost.
Whose death when I beheld, no marvel was it, right
For pity though my heart did bleed, to see so
      piteous sight.
My blood from heat to cold oft changed wonders
      sore;
A thousand troubles there I found I never knew
      before:
'Tween dread and dolour so my sprites were brought
      in fear,
That long it was ere I could call to mind what I
      did there.

But as each thing hath end, so had these pains of
    mine :
The furies past, and I my wits restor'd by length
    of time.
Then, as I could devise, to seek I thought it best
Where I might find some worthy place for such a
    corse to rest.
And in my mind it came, from thence not far away,
Where Cressid's love, king Priam's son, the wor-
    thy Troilus lay.
By him I made his tomb, in token he was true,
And, as to him belonged well, I covered it with blue.
Whose soul by angels' power departed not so soon,
But to the heavens, lo ! it fled, for to receive his
    doom.

COMPLAINT OF THE ABSENCE OF HER
LOVER, BEING UPON THE SEA.

GOOD ladies ! ye that have your pleasures
    in exile,
    Step in your foot, come, take a place,
      and mourn with me awhile :
And such as by their lords do set but little price,
Let them sit still, it skills them not what chance
    come on the dice.
But ye whom Love hath bound, by order of desire,
To love your lords, whose good deserts none other
    would require ;
Come ye yet once again, and set your foot by mine,

Whose woful plight, and sorrows great, no tongue
 may well define.
My love and lord, alas! in whom consists my
 wealth,
Hath fortune sent to pass the seas, in hazard of
 his health.
Whom I was wont t'embrace with well contented
 mind,
Is now amid the foaming floods at pleasure of the
 wind.
Where God well him preserve, and soon him home
 me send;
Without which hope my life, alas! were shortly
 at an end.
Whose absence yet, although my hope doth tell
 me plain,
With short return he comes anon, yet ceaseth not
 my pain.
The fearful dreams I have ofttimes do grieve me
 so,
That when I wake, I lie in doubt, where they be
 true or no.
Sometime the roaring seas, me seems, do grow so
 high,
That my dear lord, ay me! alas! methinks I see
 him die.
Another time the same doth tell me, he is come,
And playing, where I shall him find, with his fair
 little son.[1]

[1] In the copy printed by Dr. Nott from the Harrington
MS. this line stands,
" And playing, where I shall him find with T. his little son."
which induces that writer to observe: " This proves the piece

So forth I go apace to see that liefsome sight,
And with a kiss, methinks I say, ' Welcome, my
    lord, my knight ;
Welcome, my sweet ; alas ! the stay of my welfare ;
Thy presence bringeth forth a truce betwixt me
    and my care.'
Then lively doth he look, and salueth me again,
And saith, ' My dear, how is it now that you have
    all this pain ?'
Wherewith the heavy cares, that heap'd are in my
    breast,
Break forth and me dischargen clean, of all my
    huge unrest.
But when I me awake, and find it but a dream,
The anguish of my former woe beginneth more
    extreme ;
And me tormenteth so that unneath[1] may I find
Some hidden place, wherein to slake the gnawing
    of my mind.
Thus every way you see, with absence how I burn :
And for my wound no cure I find, but hope of
    good return :
Save when I think, by sour how sweet is felt the
    more,
It doth abate some of my pains, that I abode before.
And then unto myself I say : ' When we shall
    meet,

---

to have been written, not as an exercise of fancy, but for some
existing person." If this conjecture be correct, the Com-
plainant may have been intended for Lady Surrey, and " T.
his little son," for *Thomas* her eldest son, afterwards Duke
of Norfolk.

   [1] With difficulty.

But little while shall seem this pain ; the joy shall
    be so sweet.'
Ye winds, I you conjure, in chiefest of your rage,
That ye my lord me safely send, my sorrows to
    assuage.
And that I may not long abide in this excess,
Do your good will to cure a wight, that liveth in
    distress.

A PRAISE OF HIS LOVE,

WHEREIN HE REPROVETH THEM THAT COMPARE

THEIR LADIES WITH HIS.

GIVE place, ye lovers, here before
    That spent your boasts and brags in vain ;
    My Lady's beauty passeth more
    The best of yours, I dare well sayen,
Than doth the sun the candle light,
Or brightest day the darkest night.

And thereto hath a troth as just
As had Penelope the fair ;
For what she saith, ye may it trust,
As it by writing sealed were :
And virtues hath she many moe
Than I with pen have skill to show.

I could rehearse, if that I would,
The whole effect of Nature's plaint,

When she had lost the perfect mould,
The like to whom she could not paint :
With wringing hands, how she did cry,
And what she said, I know it, I.

I know she swore with raging mind,
Her kingdom only set apart,
There was no loss, by law of kind,
That could have gone so near her heart ;
And this was chiefly all her pain :
' She could not make the like again.'

Sith Nature thus gave her the praise,
To be the chiefest work she wrought ;
In faith, methink ! some better ways
On your behalf might well be sought,
Than to compare, as ye have done,
To match the candle with the sun.

TO HIS MISTRESS.[1]

F he that erst the form so lively drew
Of Venus' face, triumph'd in painter's
art ;
Thy Father then what glory did ensue,
By whose pencil a Goddess made thou art.
Touched with flame that figure made some rue,
And with her love surprised many a heart.
There lack'd yet that should cure their hot desire :
Thou canst inflame and quench the kindled fire.

[1] Printed for the first time by Dr. Nott, from a MS. in the possession of Mr. Hill.

TO THE LADY THAT SCORNED HER
LOVER.

ALTHOUGH I had a check,
  To give the mate is hard;
For I have found a neck,[1]
  To keep my men in guard.
And you that hardy are,
  To give so great assay
Unto a man of war,
  To drive his men away;

I rede[2] you take good heed,
  And mark this foolish verse;
For I will so provide,
  That I will have your ferse.[3]
And when your ferse is had,
  And all your war is done;
Then shall yourself be glad
  To end that you begun.

For if by chance I win
  Your person in the field;
Too late then come you in
  Yourself to me to yield.
For I will use my power,
  As captain full of might;
And such I will devour,
  As use to shew me spite.

[1] A nook.   [2] Counsel, advise.
          [3] The Queen at Chess.
                  D

And for because you gave
Me check in such degree ;
This vantage, lo ! I have,
Now check, and guard to thee.
Defend it if thou may ;
Stand stiff in thine estate :
For sure I will assay,
If I can give thee mate.

A WARNING TO THE LOVER, HOW HE IS

ABUSED BY HIS LOVE.   •

OO dearly had I bought my green and
youthful years,
If in mine age I could not find when
craft for love appears.
And seldom though I come in court among the
rest,
Yet can I judge in colours dim, as deep as can the
best.
Where grief torments the man that suff'reth secret
smart,
To break it forth unto some friend, it easeth well
the heart.
So stands it now with me, for, my beloved friend,
This case is thine, for whom I feel such torment
of my mind.
And for thy sake I burn so in my secret breast,
That till thou know my whole disease, my heart
can have no rest,

I see how thine abuse hath wrested so thy wits,
That all it yields to thy desire, and follows thee
       by fits.
Where thou hast loved so long, with heart, and all
       thy power,
I see thee fed with feigned words, thy freedom to
       devour:
I know (though she say nay, and would it well
       withstand)
When in her grace thou held thee most, she bare
       thee but in hand.
I see her pleasant chere in chiefest of thy suit;
When thou art gone, I see him come that gathers
       up the fruit.
And eke in thy respect, I see the base degree
Of him to whom she gave the heart, that promised
       was to thee.
I see, (what would you more,) stood never man so
       sure
On woman's word, but wisdom would mistrust it
       to endure.

THE FORSAKEN LOVER DESCRIBETH AND FORSAKETH LOVE.

 LOATHSOME place ! where I
Have seen, and heard my dear ;
When in my heart her eye
Hath made her thought appear,
By glimpsing with such grace,—
As fortune it ne would
That lasten any space,
Between us longer should.

As fortune did advance
To further my desire;
Even so hath fortune's chance
Thrown all amidst the mire.
And that I have deserved,
With true and faithful heart,
Is to his hands reserved,
That never felt the smart.

But happy is that man
That scaped hath the grief,
That love well teach him can,
By wanting his relief.
A scourge to quiet minds
It is, who taketh heed ;
A common plage that binds ;
A travail without meed.

This gift it hath also :
Whoso enjoys it most,
A thousand troubles grow,
To vex his wearied ghost.
And last it may not long ;
The truest thing of all :
And sure the greatest wrong,
That is within this thrall.

But since thou, desert place,
Canst give me no account
Of my desired grace,
That I to have was wont ;
Farewell ! thou hast me taught,
To think me not the first
That love hath set aloft,
And casten in the dust.

THE LOVER DESCRIBETH HIS REST-
LESS STATE.[1]

S oft as I behold, and see
The sovereign beauty that me bound ;
The nigher my comfort is to me,
Alas ! the fresher is my wound.

As flame doth quench by rage of fire,
And running streams consume by rain ;

[1] The 3rd, 6th, and 8th stanzas do not occur in Tottel's
collection, but were supplied by Dr. Nott from a copy in the
" Nugæ Antiquæ."

So doth the sight that I desire
Appease my grief, and deadly pain.

Like as the fly that seeth the flame,
And thinks to play her in the fire;
That found her woe, and sought her game
Where grief did grow by her desire.

First when I saw those crystal streams,
Whose beauty made my mortal wound;.
I little thought within their beams
So sweet a venom to have found.

But wilful will did prick me forth,
And blind Cupid did whip and guide;
Force made me take my grief in worth; [1]
My fruitless hope my harm did hide;

Wherein is hid the cruel bit,
Whose sharp repulse none can resist;
And eke the spur that strains each wit
To run the race against his list.

As cruel waves full oft be found
Against the rocks to roar and cry;
So doth thy heart full oft rebound
Against my breast full bitterly.

And as the spider draws her line,
With labour lost I frame my suit;
The fault is her's, the loss is mine:
Of ill sown seed, such is the fruit.

[1] Patiently.

I fall, and see mine own decay;
As he that bears flame in his breast,
Forgets for pain to cast away
The thing that breedeth his unrest.[1]

THE LOVER EXCUSETH HIMSELF OF

SUSPECTED CHANGE.

THOUGH I regarded not
   The promise made by me ;
Or passed not to spot
   My faith and honesty :
Yet were my fancy strange,
   And wilful will to wite,[2]
If I sought now to change
   A falcon for a kite.

All men might well dispraise
   My wit and enterprise,
If I esteemed a pese [3]
   Above a pearl in price :
Or judged the owl in sight
   The sparhawk to excel;

---

[1] In Tottel's collection this stanza is thus printed—

   I fall and see mine own decay,
   As one that bears flame in his breast;
   Forgets in pain to put away
   The thing that breedeth mine unrest.

[2] To censure.   [3] A pea.

Which flieth but in the night,
As all men know right well.

Or if I sought to sail
Into the brittle port,
Where anchor hold doth fail
To such as do resort;
And leave the haven sure,
Where blows no blustering wind;
Nor fickleness in ure,[1]
So far-forth as I find.

No! think me not so light,
Nor of so churlish kind,
Though it lay in my might
My bondage to unbind,
That I would leave the hind
To hunt the gander's foe.[2]
No! no! I have no mind
To make exchanges so.

Nor yet to change at all;
For think, it may not be
That I should seek to fall
From my felicity.
Desirous for to win,
And loth for to forego;
Or new change to begin;
How may all this be so?

The fire it cannot freeze,
For it is not his kind;

[1] Practise.   [2] The fox.

Nor true love cannot lese [1]
The constance of the mind.
Yet as soon shall the fire
Want heat to blaze and burn;
As I, in such desire,
Have once a thought to turn.

A CARELESS MAN

SCORNING AND DESCRIBING THE SUBTLE USAGE OF

WOMEN TOWARD THEIR LOVERS.

WRAPT in my careless cloak, as I walk
        to and fro,
    I see how Love can shew what force
        there reigneth in his bow:
And how he shooteth eke a hardy heart to wound;
And where he glanceth by again, that little hurt
    is found.
For seldom is it seen he woundeth hearts alike;
The one may rage, when t'other's love is often far
    to seek.
All this I see, with more; and wonder thinketh me
How he cán strike the one so sore, and leave the
    other free.
I see that wounded wight that suff'reth all this
        wrong,
How he is fed with yeas and nays, and liveth all
    too long.

[1] Lose.

In silence though I keep such secrets to myself,
Yet do I see how she sometime doth yield a look
    by stealth,
As though it seem'd; ' I wis, I will not lose thee
    so :'
When in her heart so sweet a thought did never
    truly grow.
Then say I thus : ' Alas ! that man is far from bliss,
That doth receive for his relief none other gain
    but this.'
And she, that feeds him so, I feel and find it plain,
Is but to glory in her power, that over such can
    reign.
Nor are such graces spent, but when she thinks,
    that he,
A wearied man, is fully bent such fancies to let flee.
Then to retain him still, she wrasteth new her grace,
And smileth, lo ! as though she would forthwith
    the man embrace.
But when the proof is made to try such looks withal,
He findeth then the place all void, and freighted
    full of gall.
Lord ! what abuse is this ; who can such women
    praise,
That for their glory do devise to use such crafty
    ways ?
I, that among the rest do sit and mark the row,
Find that in her is greater craft, than is in twenty
    mo' :
Whose tender years, alas ! with wiles so well are
    sped,
What will she do when hoary hairs are powder'd
    in her head ?

AN ANSWER IN THE BEHALF OF A
WOMAN.

OF AN UNCERTAIN AUTHOR.[1]

GIRT in my guiltless gown, as I sit here
    and sow,
      I see that things are not in deed, as to
      the outward show.
And who so list to look and note things somewhat
    near,
Shall find where plainness seems to haunt, nothing
    but craft appear.
For with indifferent eyes myself can well discern,
How some to guide a ship in storms stick not[2] to
    take the stern ;
Whose skill and courage tried [3] in calm to steer a
    barge,
They would soon shew, you should foresee,[4] it were
    too great a charge.
And some I see again sit still and say but small,

[1] This poem was printed as in the text by Dr. Nott, from the Harrington MS., which alone contains the last eighteen lines. The variations between that copy and the printed editions are pointed out in the notes. The remark in Tottel's Collection that it was by " an uncertain author " justifies a doubt whether it was written by Surrey. It is there entitled " Of the Dissembling Lover."

[2] seek for.   [3] Whose practice if were proved.
[4] Assuredly believe it well.

That can [1] do ten times more than they that say
    they can do all.
Whose goodly gifts are such, the more they un-
    derstand,
The more they seek to learn and know, and take
    less charge in hand.
And to declare more plain, the time flits not so
    fast,
But I can bear right [2] well in mind the song now
    sung, and past;
The author whereof came, wrapt in a crafty cloak,
In [3] will to force a flaming fire where he could
    raise no smoke.
If power and will had met, [4] as it appeareth plain,
The [5] truth nor right had ta'en no place; their
    virtues had been vain.
So that you may perceive, and I may safely see,
The innocent that guiltless is, condemned should
    have be.
Much like untruth to this the story doth declare,
Where the Elders laid to Susan's charge meet
    matter to compare.
They did her both accuse, and eke condemn her
    too,
And yet no reason, right, nor truth, did lead them
    so to do!
And she thus judg'd to die, toward her death went
    forth,
Fraughted with faith, a patient pace, taking her
    wrong in worth.
But He that doth defend all those that in him trust,

---

[1] could   [2] full.   [3] With.   [4] join'd.   [5] Then.

Did raise a child for her defence to shield her from
　　th' unjust.
And Daniel chosen was then of his wrong to
　　weet,
How, in what place, and eke with whom she did
　　this crime commit.　　　　.
He caused the Elders part the one from th' other's
　　sight,
And did examine one by one, and charg'd them
　　both say right.
' Under a mulberry tree it was ;' first said the one.
The next named a pomegranate tree, whereby the
　　truth was known.
Then Susan was discharg'd, and they condemn'd
　　to die,
As right requir'd, and they deserv'd, that fram'd
　　so foul a lie.
And He that her preserv'd, and lett them of their
　　lust,
Hath me defended hitherto, and will do still I trust.

THE CONSTANT LOVER LAMENTETH.

SINCE fortune's wrath envieth the wealth
　　Wherein I reigned, by the sight
　　Of that, that fed mine eyes by stealth
　　With sour, sweet, dread, and delight ;
Let not my grief move you to moan,
For I will weep and wail alone.

Spite drave me into Boreas' reign,[1]
Where hoary frosts the fruits do bite,
When hills were spread, and every plair
With stormy winter's mantle white;
And yet, my dear, such was my heat,
When others froze, then did I sweat.

And now, though on the sun I drive,
Whose fervent flame all things decays;
His beams in brightness may not strive
With light of your sweet golden rays;
Nor from my breast this heat remove
The frozen thoughts, graven by Love.

Ne may the waves of the salt flood
Quench that your beauty set on fire;
For though mine eyes forbear the food,
That did relieve the hot desire;
Such as I was, such will I be;
Your own; what would ye more of me?

[1] Her anger drove me into a colder climate

A SONG WRITTEN BY THE EARL OF SURREY,

OF A LADY THAT REFUSED TO DANCE WITH HIM.[1]

EACH beast can choose his fere accord-
  ing to his mind,
  And eke can shew a friendly chere,
  like to their beastly kind.
A Lion saw I late, as white as any snow,
Which seemed well to lead the race, his port the
  same did show.
Upon the gentle beast to gaze it pleased me,
For still me thought he seemed well of noble blood
  to be.

[1] Dr. Nott's remark on this piece, "That it is valuable from the circumstance of its preserving an account of a quarrel between Surrey and the fair Geraldine, which, as we hear nothing of any reconciliation afterwards, was the occasion probably of his renouncing his ill-fated passion," is an amusing instance of first imagining a fact, and then making every circumstance support it. The learned editor, as in most other instances, assumes that Geraldine was the subject of the poem, without a shadow of evidence; and gratuitously gives it this title—"Surrey renounces all affection for the fair Geraldine," whereas, in all the printed editions, it bears the title assigned to it in the text. There is no doubt that Surrey personated himself by the "White Lion," which was one of the badges (and not the arms, as Dr. Nott asserts) of the house of Howard, derived from their descent from the Mowbrays, Dukes of Norfolk. The word "pranceth" in line 7, alluded to the position "rampant" of the animal, and

And as he pranced before, still seeking for a make,
As who would say, ' There is none here, I trow,
     will me forsake.'
I might perceive a Wolf as white as whalèsbone ;
A fairer beast of fresher hue, beheld I never none;
Save that her looks were coy, and froward eke her
     grace :
Unto the which this gentle beast 'gan him advance
     apace.
And with a beck full low he bowed at her feet,
In humble wise, as who would say, ' I am too far
     unmeet.'
But such a scornful chere, wherewith she him re-
     warded !
Was never seen, I trow, the like, to such as well
     deserved.
With that she start aside well near a foot or twain,
And unto him thus 'gan she say, with spite and
     great disdain :

perhaps a playful reference was intended to Surrey's invita-
tion to the lady to *dance.* But there is not any reason to
presume that by the *Wolf* the fair Geraldine was intended,
though it is almost certain that the family of the lady adverted to bore that animal on their standards, or in their
arms. Dr. Nott has cited a MS. in the Museum to prove
that the Fitzgeralds, Earls of Kildare, used a Wolf as their
crest, but this is unsupported by any other authority, and
Drayton, with more probability, says, that the lady meant
by the " Wolf," was Ann, the daughter of Sir Edward Stanhope, who became the wife of the Protector Somerset. The
Stanhope family once used a Wolf as their crest, in consequence of their descent from Maulovel, and a Wolf is still one
of the supporters of the Earls of Chesterfield, Stanhope, and
Harrington. See Collins' Peerage, ed. 1779, iii. 301, 302.
It is proper to add, that the family of Arundell of Lanhearne,
in Cornwall, bore a white wolf as a badge.

'Lion,' she said, ' if thou hadst known my mind
    before,
Thou hadst not spent thy travail thus, nor all thy
    pain for-lore.
Do way ! I let thee weet,[1] thou shalt not play with
    me :
Go range about, where thou mayst find some
    meeter fere for thee.'
With that he beat his tail, his eyes began to flame;
I might perceive his noble heart much moved by
    the same.
Yet saw I him refrain, and eke his wrath assuage,
And unto her thus 'gan he say, when he was past
    his rage :
' Cruel ! you do me wrong, to set me thus so light ;
Without desert for my good will to shew me such
    despite.
How can ye thus intreat a Lion of the race,
That with his paws a crowned king devoured in
    the place.[2]
Whose nature is to prey upon no simple food,
As long as he may suck the flesh, and drink of
    noble blood.
If you be fair and fresh, am I not of your hue ?[3]
And for my vaunt I dare well say, my blood is
    not untrue.

---

[1] I let thee know.

[2] Apparently an allusion to the defeat and death of James the Fourth at Flodden Field, by Thomas, then Earl of Surrey, the Poet's grandfather.

[3] Query, is it to be understood by this line that Surrey was related to the lady, or did he only mean that his lion was of the same hue as her wolf ?

E

For you yourself have heard, it is not long ago,
Sith that for love one of the race did end his life
      in woe,
In tower strong and high, for his assured truth,
Whereas in tears he spent his breath, alas ! the
      more the ruth.
This gentle beast so died, whom nothing could
      remove,
But willingly to lese his life for loss of his true
      love.[1]
Other there be whose lives do linger still in pain,
Against their wills preserved are, that would have
      died fain.
But now I do perceive that nought it moveth you,
My good intent, my gentle heart, nor yet my kind
      so true.
But that your will is such to lure me to the trade,

---

[1] Dr. Nott observes: "This means Thomas Howard, second son of Thomas second Duke of Norfolk, by Agnes his second wife, and consequently half uncle to Surrey. He was attainted of high treason, and committed to the Tower, in June 1536, for having, without the knowledge or approbation of King Henry VIII, affianced himself to the Lady Margaret Douglas, daughter of Margaret Queen of Scotland, the King's sister. Lord Thomas Howard remained in confinement till his decease on Allhallows Eve, 1538. Upon his death the Lady Margaret, who had been confined likewise, was set at liberty. It is probable that this unfortunate affiance was the effect on the part of Lord Thomas Howard, as well as on the part of the Lady Margaret, of real attachment, and not of ambition. Had he relinquished all claim to her hand, he probably would have been released from his confinement. It is likely therefore that his love, as Surrey intimates, really cost him his life."

As other some full many years to trace by craft ye
    made.
And thus behold our kinds, how that we differ far;
I seek my foes; and you your friends do threaten
    still with war.
I fawn where I am fled; you slay, that seeks to
    you;
I can devour no yielding prey; you kill where
    you subdue.
My kind is to desire the honour of the field;
And you with blood to slake your thirst on such
    as to you yield.
Wherefore I would you wist, that for your coyed
    looks,
I am no man that will be trapp'd, nor tangled
    with such hooks.
And though some lust to love, where blame full
    well they might;
And to such beasts of current sought, that should
    have travail bright;
I will observe the law that Nature gave to me,
To conquer such as will resist, and let the rest go
    free.
And as a falcon free, that soareth in the air,
Which never fed on hand nor lure; nor for no
    stale[1] doth care;
While that I live and breathe, such shall my cus-
    tom be
In wildness of the woods to seek my prey, where
    pleaseth me;

[1] A piece of meat used to allure falcons back to their
master.

Where many one shall rue, that never made
    offence :
Thus your refuse against my power shall boot
    them no defence.
And for revenge thereof I vow and swear thereto,
A thousand spoils I shall commit I never thought
    to do.
And if to light on you my luck so good shall be,
I shall be glad to feed on that, that would have
    fed on me.
And thus farewell, Unkind, to whom I bent and
    bow ;
I would you wist, the ship is safe that bare his
    sails so low.
Sith that a Lion's heart is for a Wolf no prey,
With bloody mouth go slake your thirst on simple
    sheep, I say,
With more despite and ire than I can now express;
Which to my pain though I refrain, the cause you
    may well guess.
As for because myself was author of the game,
It boots me not that for my wrath I should disturb
    the same.'

THE FAITHFUL LOVER

DECLARETH HIS PAINS AND HIS UNCERTAIN JOYS,

AND WITH ONLY HOPE RECOMFORTETH

SOMEWHAT HIS WOEFUL HEART.

F care do cause men cry, why do not I
   complain ?
 If each man do bewail his woe, why
   shew I not my pain ?
Since that amongst them all, I dare well say is none
So far from weal, so full of woe, or hath more
   cause to moan.
For all things having life, sometime hath quiet rest;
The bearing ass, the drawing ox, and every other
   beast ;
The peasant and the post, that serve at all assays ;
The ship-boy and the galley-slave, have time to
   take their ease ;
Save I, alas ! whom care, of force doth so constrain,
To wail the day, and wake the night, continually
   in pain.
From pensiveness to plaint, from plaint to bitter
   tears,
From tears to painful plaint again ; and thus my
   life it wears.
No thing under the sun, that I can hear or see,
But moveth me for to bewail my cruel destiny.

For where men do rejoice, since that I cannot so,
I take no pleasure in that place, it doubleth but
    my woe.
And when I hear the sound of song or instrument,
Methink each tune there doleful is, and helps me
    to lament.
And if I see some have their most desired sight,
' Alas ! ' think I, ' each man hath weal save I, most
    woful wight.'
Then as the stricken deer withdraws himself alone,
So do I seek some secret place, where I may make
    my moan.
There do my flowing eyes shew forth my melting
    heart ;
So that the streams of those two wells right well
    declare my smart.
And in those cares so cold, I force myself a heat
(As sick men in their shaking fits procure them-
    selves to sweat)
With thoughts, that for the time do much appease
    my pain :
But yet they cause a farther fear, and breed my
    woe again.
Methink within my thought I see right plain ap-
    pear
My heart's delight, my sorrow's leech, mine earthly
    goddess here,
With every sundry grace, that I have seen her have,
Thus I within my woful breast her picture paint
    and grave.
And in my thought I roll her beauties to and fro ;
Her laughing chere, her lovely look, my heart that
    pierced so.

Her strangeness when I sued her servant for to be ;
And what she said, and how she smiled, when
    that she pitied me.
Then comes a sudden fear that riveth[1] all my rest,
Lest absence cause forgetfulness to sink within her
    breast.
For when I think how far this earth doth us divide,
Alas ! me-seems love throws me down ; I feel how
    that I slide.
But then I think again, 'Why should I thus mistrust
So sweet a wight, so sad and wise, that is so true
    and just ?
For loath she was to love, and wavering is she not ;
The farther off the more desired.' Thus lovers
    tie their knot.
So in despair and hope plung'd am I both up and
    down,
As is the ship with wind and wave, when Neptune
    list to frown :
But as the watery showers delay the raging wind,
So doth Good-hope clean put away despair out of
    my mind ;
And bids me for to serve, and suffer patiently :
For what wot I the after weal that fortune wills
    to me.
For those that care do know, and tasted have of
    trouble,
When passed is their woful pain, each joy shall
    seem them double.
And bitter sends she now, to make me taste the
    better

       [1] To tear, to rend asunder.

The pleasant sweet, when that it comes, to make
    it seem the sweeter.
And so determine I to serve until my breath;
Yea, rather die a thousand times, than once to
    false my faith.
And if my feeble corpse, through weight of woful
    smart
Do fail, or faint, my will it is that still she keep
    my heart.
And when this carcass here to earth shall be re-
    far'd,[1]
I do bequeath my wearied ghost to serve her after-
    ward.

THE MEANS TO ATTAIN HAPPY LIFE.

ARTIAL, the things that do attain
    The happy life, be these, I find:
    The riches left, not got with pain;
    The fruitful ground, the quiet mind:

The equal friend, no grudge, no strife;
No charge of rule, nor governance;
Without disease, the healthful life;
The household of continuance:

The mean[2] diet, no delicate[3] fare;
True wisdom join'd with simpleness;

[1] Referred, to bring back.   [2] Moderate.
    [3] Dainty, in one MS.

The night discharged of all care,
Where wine the wit may not oppress :

The faithful wife, without debate ;
Such sleeps as may beguile the night :
Contented with thine own estate ;
Ne wish for death, ne fear his might.

PRAISE OF MEAN AND CONSTANT ESTATE.

F thy life, Thomas,[1] this compass well
  mark :
  Not aye with full sails the high seas to
  beat ;
Ne by coward dread, in shunning storms dark,
On shallow shores thy keel in peril freat.[2]

Whoso gladly halseth[3] the golden mean,
Void of dangers advisedly hath his home ;
Not with loathsome muck as a den unclean,
Nor palace like, whereat disdain may glome.[4]

The lofty pine the great wind often rives ;
With violenter sway fallen turrets steep ;
Lightnings assault the high mountains and clives.[5]
A heart well stay'd, in overthwartes[6] deep.

[1] Sir Thomas Wyatt.   [2] Damage.
[3] Embraceth.   [4] Look at scornfully.
[5] Steep cliffs.   [6] Adverse fortunes.

Hopeth amends : in sweet, doth fear the sour.
God that sendeth, withdraweth winter sharp.
Now ill, not aye thus : once Phœbus to low'r,
With bow unbent, shall cease and frame to harp

His voice; in strait estate appear thou stout;
And so wisely, when lucky gale of wind
All thy puft sails shall fill, look well about;
Take in a reef : haste is waste, proof doth find.

PRAISE OF CERTAIN PSALMS OF DAVID,

TRANSLATED BY SIR THOMAS [WYATT]

THE ELDER.

HE great Macedon, that out of Persia
        chased
    Darius, of whose huge power all Asia
        rung ;
In the rich ark[1] Dan Homer's rhymes he placed,
Who feigned gests[2] of heathen princes sung.
What holy grave, what worthy sepulture,
To Wyatt's Psalms should Christians then pur-
    chàse ?
Where he doth paint the lively faith, and pure,
The steadfast hope, the sweet return to grace,
Of just David, by perfect penitence ;
Where rulers may see in a mirror clear,

---

[1] Chest.   [2] Heroic deeds.

The bitter fruit of false concupiscence ;
How Jewry bought Urias' death full dear.
   In Princes' hearts God's scourge imprinted deep,
   Ought them awake out of their sinful sleep.[1]

OF THE DEATH OF SIR THOMAS WYATT.

 IVERS thy death do diversely bemoan:
      Some, that in presence of thy livelihed[2]
      Lurked, whose breasts envy with hate
         had swoln,
Yield Cæsar's tears upon Pompeius' head.
Some, that watched with the murd'rer's knife,
With eager thirst to drink thy guiltless blood,
Whose practice brake by happy end of life,
With envious tears to hear thy fame so good.
But I, that knew what harbour'd in that head ;
What virtues rare were tempered in that breast ;
Honour the place that such a jewel bred,
And kiss the ground whereas the corpse doth rest ;
   With vapour'd eyes : from whence such streams
      availe,[3]
   As Pyramus did on Thisbe's breast bewail.

[1] Mr. Warton thinks that "probably the last lines may
contain an oblique allusion to some of the amours of King
Henry VIII."
 [2] Being alive.   [3] Fall down.

OF THE SAME.

WYATT resteth here, that quick[1] could
    never rest :   .
    Whose heavenly gifts increased by
      disdain ;
And virtue sank the deeper in his breast :
Such profit he by envy could obtain.
A head, where wisdom mysteries did frame ;
Whose hammers beat still in that lively brain,
As on a stithe,[2] where that some work of fame
Was daily wrought, to turn to Britain's gain.
A visage, stern and mild ; where both did grow
Vice to contemn, in virtue to rejoice :
Amid great storms, whom grace assured so,
To live upright, and smile at Fortune's choice.
A hand, that taught what might be said in rhyme;
That reft Chaucer the glory of his wit.
A mark, the which (unperfected for time)
Some may approach, but never none shall hit.
A tongue, that serv'd in foreign realms his king ;
Whose courteous talk to virtue did inflame
Each noble heart ; a worthy guide to bring
Our English youth, by travail, unto fame.
An eye, whose judgment none affect[3] could blind,
Friends to allure, and foes to reconcile ;
Whose piercing look did represent a mind
With virtue fraught, reposed, void of guile.
A heart, where dread was never so imprest
To hide the thought that might the truth advance;

---

[1] Alive.   [2] Forge, or anvil.   [3] Passion.

In neither fortune loft,[1] nor yet represt,
To swell in wealth, or yield unto mischance.
A valiant corpse, where force and beauty met:
Happy, alas! too happy, but for foes,
Lived, and ran the race that Nature set;
Of manhood's shape, where she the mould did lose.
But to the heavens that simple soul is fled,
Which left, with such as covet Christ to know,
Witness of faith, that never shall be dead;
Sent for our health, but not received so.
Thus, for our guilt this jewel have we lost;
The earth his bones, the heavens possess his ghost.

OF THE SAME.

N the rude age, when knowledge was
    not rife,
   If Jove in Crete, and other were that
    taught
Arts, to convert to profit of our life,
Wend after death to have their temples sought:
If, Virtue yet no void unthankful time
Failed of some to blast her endless fame;
(A goodly mean both to deter from crime,
And to her steps our sequel to inflame)
In days of truth if Wyatt's friends then wail
(The only debt that dead of quick may claim)
That rare wit spent, employ'd to our avail,
Where Christ is taught, we led to Virtue's train.
  His lively face their breasts how did it freat,
  Whose cinders yet with envy they do eat.

[1] Elevated.

AN EPITAPH ON CLERE,

SURREY'S FAITHFUL FRIEND AND FOLLOWER.[1]

ORFOLK sprung thee, Lambeth holds
thee dead;
Clere, of the Count of Cleremont, thou
hight!
Within the womb of Ormond's race thou bred,
And saw'st thy cousin crowned in thy sight.
Shelton for love, Surrey for lord.thou chase;[2]
(Aye, me! whilst life did last that league was tender)

[1] These lines were inscribed, with the epitaph above, on
a table in Lambeth Church:
"Epitaphium Thomæ Clere, qui fato functus est 1545,
auctore Henrico Howard, Comite Surrey. In cujus faelicis
ingenii specimen, et singularis facundiae argumentum, ap-
pensa faut haec Tabula per W. Howard, filium Thomae
nuper Ducis Norfolciensis, filii ejusdem Henrici Comitis."
This epitaph occurs, with some trifling variations, in
Camden's *Remains*, Aubrey's *History of Surrey*, v. 247, and
in Bloomfield's *Norfolk*. Thomas Clere was the youngest
son of Sir Robert Clere, of Ormesby in Norfolk, (the descen-
dant of Clere, of Cleremont in Normandy) by Alice, daughter
of Sir William Boleyn, by Margaret, daughter and coheir of
Thomas Boteler, Earl of Ormond. He was consequently
first "cousin" of Queen Anne Boleyn, whom "he saw
crowned" in 1533, and was connected with "Ormond's race."
"Shelton" is presumed to have been a daughter of Sir John
Shelton, of Shelton in Norfolk, but it does not appear that
Clere married her. He died on the 14th of April, 1545, and
was buried at Lambeth. These facts explain most of the
allusions in the epitaph, and the others are noticed in the
Memoir of Surrey.

[2] Didst choose.

Tracing whose steps thou sawest Kelsal blaze,
Landrecy burnt, and batter'd Boulogne render.[1]
At Montreuil gates, hopeless of all recure,[2]
Thine Earl, half dead, gave in thy hand his will;
Which cause did thee this pining death procure,
Ere summers four times seven thou couldst fulfill.
 Ah! Clere! if love had booted care or cost,
 Heaven had not won, nor earth so timely lost.

OF SARDANAPALUS'S DISHONORABLE

LIFE AND MISERABLE DEATH.

TH' Assyrian king, in peace, with foul
   desire
  And filthy lusts that stain'd his regal
   heart;
In war, that should set princely hearts on fire,
Did yield, vanquisht for want of martial art.
The dint of swords from kisses seemed strange;
And harder than his lady's side, his targe:[3]
From glutton feasts to soldier's fare, a change;
His helmet, far above a garland's charge:
Who scarce the name of manhood did retain,
Drenched in sloth and womanish delight:
Feeble of spirit, impatient of pain,
When he had lost his honour, and his right,
 (Proud time of wealth, in storms appalled with
   dread,)
 Murder'd himself, to shew some manful deed.

[1] Surrender. [2] Recovery. [3] Shield.

HOW NO AGE IS CONTENT

WITH HIS OWN ESTATE, AND HOW THE AGE OF CHILDREN IS THE HAPPIEST IF THEY HAD SKILL TO UNDERSTAND IT.

LAID in my quiet bed, in study as I
    were,
    I saw within my troubled head a heap
    of thoughts appear.
And every thought did shew so lively in mine eyes,
That now I sigh'd, and then I smiled, as cause of
    thought did rise.
I saw the little boy in thought how oft that he
Did wish of God, to scape the rod, a tall young man
    to be.
The young man eke that feels his bones with pains
    opprest,
How he would be a rich old man, to live and lie
    at rest.
The rich old man that sees his end draw on so
    sore,
How he would be a boy again, to live so much the
    more.
Whereat full oft I smiled, to see how all these three,
From boy to man, from man to boy, would chop
    and change degree.
And musing thus I think, the case is very strange,

That man from wealth, to live in woe, doth ever
    seek to change.
Thus thoughtful as I lay, I saw my wither'd skin,
How it doth shew my dented chews, the flesh was
    worn so thin.
And eke my toothless chaps, the gates of my right
    way,
That opes and shuts as I do speak, do thus unto
    me say:
' Thy white and hoarish hairs, the messengers of
    age,
That shew, like lines of true belief, that this life
    doth assuage ;
Bid thee lay hand, and feel them hanging on thy
    chin ;
The which do write two ages past, the third now
    coming in.
Hang up therefore the bit of thy young wanton time:
And thou that therein beaten art, the happiest life
    define.'
Whereat I sigh'd, and said: ' Fare well ! my wonted
    joy ;
Truss up thy pack, and trudge from me to every
    little boy ;
And tell them thus from me; their time most happy
    is,
If, to their time, they reason had, to know the truth
    of this.'

F

BONUM EST MIHI QUOD HUMILIASTI ME.

HE storms are past; the clouds are over-
      blown ;
And humble chere great rigour hath
      represt.
For the default is set a pain foreknown ;
And patience graft in a determined breast.
And in the heart, where heaps of griefs were grown,
The sweet revenge hath planted mirth and rest.
No company so pleasant as mine own.

   .   .   .   .   .   .

Thraldom at large hath made this prison free.
Danger well past, remembered, works delight.
Of ling'ring doubts such hope is sprung, pardie ![1]
That nought I find displeasant in my sight,
But when my glass presented unto me
The cureless wound, that bleedeth day and night,
To think, alas ! such hap should granted be
Unto a wretch, that hath no heart to fight,
   To spill that blood, that hath so oft been shed,
   For Britain's sake, alas ! and now is dead !

[1] A corruption of *par Dieu.*

EXHORTATION TO LEARN BY OTHERS' TROUBLE.

MY Ratclif,[1] when thy rechless[2] youth
    offends,
    Receive thy scourge by others' chastise-
        ment;
For such calling, when it works none amends,
Then plagues are sent without advertisement.
Yet Solomon said, the wronged shall recure:
But Wyatt said true; ' The scar doth aye endure.'

THE FANCY OF A WEARIED LOVER.

THE fancy, which that I have served long
    That hath alway been enemy to mine
        ease;
    Seemed of late to rue upon my wrong,
And bade me fly the cause of my misease.
And I forthwith did press out of the throng,
That thought by flight my painful heart to please
Some other way, till I saw faith more strong;
And to myself I said, ' Alas! those days
In vain were spent, to run the race so long.'

[1] Perhaps Sir Humphrey Ratcliffe, one of the gentlemen pensioners.
[2] Careless.

And with that thought I met my guide, that plain,
Out of the way wherein I wander'd wrong,
Brought me amidst the hills in base Bullayne :
   Where I am now, as restless to remain
   Against my will, full pleased with my pain.

A SATIRE AGAINST THE CITIZENS OF
LONDON.[1]

ONDON! hast thou accused me
   Of breach of laws? the root of strife?
   Within whose breast did boil to see,
   So fervent hot, thy dissolute life;
That even the hate of sins, that grow
Within thy wicked walls so rife,
For to break forth did convert so,
That terror could it not repress.
The which, by words, since preachers know
What hope is left for to redress,
By unknown means it liked me
My hidden burthen to express.
Whereby it might appear to thee
That secret sin hath secret spite;
From justice' rod no fault is free
But that all such as work unright

---

[1] " A Satire on London " was first published by Mr. Park
from a manuscript in his possession. The version printed
by Dr. Nott was collated from Park's copy and Dr. Harrington's manuscript. It was probably written after Lord
Surrey had been condemned by a London jury.

In most quiet, are next ill rest.
In secret silence of the night
This made me, with a rechless breast,
To wake thy sluggards with my bow:
A figure of the Lord's behest;
Whose scourge for sin the Scriptures shew.
That as the fearful thunder's clap
By sudden flame at hand we know;
Of pebble stones the soundless rap,
The dreadful plague might make thee see
Of God's wrath, that doth thee enwrap.
That pride might know, from conscience free,
How lofty works may her defend;
And envy find, as he hath sought,
How other seek him to offend:
And wrath taste of each cruel thought,
The just shape higher in the end:
And idle sloth, that never wrought,
To heaven his spirit lift may begin:
And greedy lucre live in dread,
To see what hate ill got goods win.
The letchers, ye that lusts do feed,
Perceive what secrecy is in sin:
And gluttons' hearts for sorrow bleed,
Awaked, when their fault they find,
In loathsome vice each drunken wight,
To stir to God this was my mind.
Thy windows had done me no spight;
But proud people that dread no fall,
Clothed with falsehood, and unright
Bred in the closures of thy wall.
But wrested to wrath in fervent zeal
Thou hast to strife, my secret call.

Indured hearts no warning feel.
O! shameless whore! is dread then gone?
Be such thy foes, as meant thy weal?
O! member of false Babylon!
The shop of craft! the den of ire!
Thy dreadful doom draws fast upon.
Thy martyrs' blood by sword and fire,
In heaven and earth for justice call.
The Lord shall hear their just desire!
The flame of wrath shall on thee fall!
With famine and pest lamentably
Stricken shall be thy lechers all.
Thy proud towers and turrets high,
Enemies to God, beat stone from stone:
Thine idols burnt that wrought iniquity:
When none thy ruin shall bemoan;
But render unto the righteous Lord,
That so hath judged Babylon,
Immortal praise with one accord.

THE LOVER DESCRIBETH HIS WHOLE STATE UNTO HIS LOVE,

AND PROMISING HER HIS FAITHFUL GOOD WILL,

ASSURETH HIMSELF OF HERS AGAIN.[1]

THE Sun, when he hath spread his rays,
And shew'd his face ten thousand ways;
Ten thousand things do then begin,
To shew the life that they are in.
The heaven shews lively art and hue,
Of sundry shapes and colours new,
And laughs upon the earth; anon,
The earth, as cold as any stone,
Wet in the tears of her own kind,
'Gins then to take a joyful mind.
For well she feels that out and out
The sun doth warm her round about,
And dries her children tenderly;
And shews them forth full orderly.
The mountains high, and how they stand!
The valleys, and the great main land!
The trees, the herbs, the towers strong,
The castles, and the rivers long!

---

[1] This poem is among those of "Uncertain Authors" printed by Tottel. Dr. Nott ascribes it to Surrey, on the authority of Turberville, in the following line:—

"Though noble Surrey said 'that absence wonders
    frame.'"

And even for joy thus of this heat
She sheweth forth her pleasures great,
And sleeps no more; but sendeth forth
Her clergions,[1] her own dear worth,
To mount and fly up to the air;
Where then they sing in order fair,
And tell in song full merrily,
How they have slept full quietly
That night, about their mother's sides.
And when they have sung more besides,
Then fall they to their mother's breasts,
Whereas they feed, or take their rests.
The hunter then sounds out his horn,
And rangeth straight through wood and corn.
On hills then shew the ewe and lamb,
And every young one with his dam.
Then lovers walk and tell their tale,
Both of their bliss, and of their bale;[2]
And how they serve, and how they do,
And how their lady loves them too.
Then tune the birds their harmony;
Then flock the fowl in company;
Then every thing doth pleasure find
In that, that comforts all their kind.
No dreams do drench them of the night
Of foes, that would them slay, or bite,
As hounds, to hunt them at the tail;
Or men force them through hill and dale.
The sheep then dreams not of the wolf:
The shipman forces not the gulf;
The lamb thinks not the butcher's knife
Should then bereave him of his life.

[1] Young brood.   [2] Sorrow

For when the sun doth once run in,
Then all their gladness doth begin;
And then their skips, and then their play:
So falls their sadness then away.
   And thus all things have comforting
In that, that doth them comfort bring;
Save I, alas! whom neither sun,
Nor aught that God hath wrought and done
May comfort aught; as though I were
A thing not made for comfort here.
For being absent from your sight,
Which are my joy and whole delight,
My comfort, and my pleasure too,
How can I joy! how should I do?
May sick men laugh, that roar with pain?
Joy they in song, that do complain?
Are martyrs in their torments glad?
Do pleasures please them that are mad?
Then how may I in comfort be,
That lack the thing should comfort me?
The blind man oft, that lacks his sight,
Complains not most the lack of light;
But those that knew their perfectness,
And then do miss their blissfulness,
In martyrs' tunes they sing, and wail
The want of that, which doth them fail.
   And hereof comes that in my brains
So many fancies work my pains.
For when I weigh your worthiness
Your wisdom, and your gentleness,
Your virtues and your sundry grace,
And mind the countenance of your face;
And how that you are she alone,

To whom I must both plain and moan;
Whom I do love, and must do still;
Whom I embrace, and aye so will,
To serve and please you as I can,
As may a woful faithful man;
And find myself so far you fro,
God knows, what torment and what woe,
My rueful heart doth then embrace;
The blood then changeth in my face;
My sinews dull, in dumps¹ I stand,
No life I feel in foot nor hand,
As pale as any clout, and dead.
Lo! suddenly the blood o'erspread,
And gone again, it nill² so bide;
And thus from life to death I slide,
As cold sometimes as any stone;
And then again as hot anon.
    Thus comes and goes my sundry fits,
To give me sundry sorts of wits;
Till that a sigh becomes my friend,
And then too all this woe doth end.
And sure, I think, that sigh doth run
From me to you, where ay you won
For well I find it easeth me;
And certès much it pleaseth me,
To think that it doth come to you,
As, would to God, it could so do.
For then I know you would soon find,
By scent and savour of the wind,
That even a martyr's sigh it is,
Whose joy you are, and all his bliss;
His comfort and his pleasure eke,

¹ Dulness of spirits.   ² Unwilling.

And even the same that he doth seek;
The same that he doth wish and crave;
The same that he doth trust to have;
To tender you in all he may,
And all your likings to obey,
As far as in his power shall lie;
Till death shall dart him for to die.

But, well-away! mine own most best,
My joy, my comfort, and my rest;
The causer of my woe and smart,
And yet the pleaser of my heart;
And she that on the earth above
Is even the worthiest for to love,
Hear now my plaint! hear now my woe!
Hear now his pain that loves you so!
And if your heart do pity bear,
Pity the cause that you shall hear.

A doleful foe in all this doubt,
Who leaves me not, but seeks me out,
Of wretched form and loathsome face,
While I stand in this woful case,
Comes forth, and takes me by the hand,
And says, 'Friend, hark! and understand;
I see well by thy port and chere,
And by thy looks and thy manere,
And by thy sadness as thou goest,
And by the sighs that thou out throwest,
That thou art stuffed full of woe.
The cause, I think, I do well know.
A fantaser thou art of some,
By whom thy wits are overcome.
But hast thou read old pamphlets aught?
Or hast thou known how books have taught

That love doth use to such as thou?
When they do think them safe enow,
And certain of their ladies' grace,
Hast thou not seen ofttimes the case,
That suddenly their hap hath turn'd?
As things in flame consum'd and burn'd.
Some by deceit forsaken right;
Some likewise changed of fancy light;
And some by absence soon forgot?
The lots in love, why knowest thou not?
And though that she be now thine own,
And knows thee well, as may be known;
And thinks thee to be such a one
As she likes best to be her own;
Think'st thou that others have not grace,
To shew and plain their woful case?
And choose her for their lady now;
And swear her truth as well as thou?
And what if she do alter mind,
Where is the love that thou wouldst find?
Absence, my friend, works wonders oft;
Now brings full low that lay full loft;
Now turns the mind, now to, now fro,
And where art thou, if it were so?'
  ' If absence,' quoth I, ' be marvellous,
I find her not so dangerous;
For she may not remove me fro.
The poor good will that I do owe
To her, whom unneth[1] I love, and shall;
And chosen have above them all,
To serve and be her own as far
As any man may offer her;

         [1] With distress.

And will her serve and will her love,
And lowly, as it shall behove;
And die her own, if fate be so:
Thus shall my heart nay part her fro.
And witness shall my good will be,
That absence takes her not from me;
But that my love doth still increase
To mind her still, and never cease:
And what I feel to be in me,
The same good will, I think, hath she;
As firm and fast to bidden aye,
Till death depart us both away.'
　　And as I have my tale thus told,
Steps unto me, with countenance bold,
A steadfast friend, a counsellor,
And nam'd is, Hope, my comforter;
And stoutly then he speaks and says,
' Thou hast said truth withouten nays;
For I assure thee, even by oath,
And thereon take my hand and troth,
That she is one the worthiest,
The truest and the faithfullest;
The gentlest and the meekest of mind,
That here on earth a man may find:
And if that love and truth were gone,
In her it might be found alone;
For in her mind no thought there is,
But how she may be true, I wis;[1]
And tenders thee, and all thy heale,[2]
And wisheth both thy health and weal;

[1] To know, perceive.
[2] Or *hele*, prosperity, happiness.

And loves thee even as far-forth than
As any woman may a man ;
And is thine own, and so she says ;
And cares for thee ten thousand ways.
On thee she speaks, on thee she thinks ;
With thee she eats, with thee she drinks ;
With thee she talks, with thee she moans ;
With thee she sighs, with thee she groans ;
With thee she says, ' Farewell, mine own !'
When thou, God knows, full far art gone.
And even, to tell thee all aright,
To thee she says full oft, ' Good night !'
And names thee oft her own most dear,
Her comfort, weal, and all her cheer ;
And tells her pillow all the tale
How thou hast done her woe and bale ;
And how she longs, and plains for thee,
And says, ' Why art thou so from me ?
Am I not she that loves thee best ?
Do I not wish thine ease and rest ?
Seek I not how I may thee please ?
Why art thou then so from thine ease ?
If I be she for whom thou carest,
For whom in torments so thou farest,
Alas ! thou knowest to find me here,
Where I remain thine own most dear ;
Thine own most true, thine own most just ;
Thine own that loves thee still, and must ;
Thine own that cares alone for thee,
As thou, I think, dost care for me ;
And even the woman, she alone
That is full bent to be thine own.'
   ' What wilt thou more ? what canst thou crave ?

Since she is as thou wouldst her have.
Then set this drivel out of door,
That in thy brains such tales doth pour,
Of absence, and of changes strange ;
Send him to those that use to change :
For she is none I thee avow,
And well thou mayst believe me now.'
  When Hope hath thus his reason said,
Lord ! how I feel me well a-paid !
A new blood then o'erspreads my bones
That all in joy I stand at ones.
My hands I throw to heav'n above,
And humbly thank the god of love ;
That of his grace I should bestow
My love so well as I it owe.
And all the planets as they stand,
I thank them too with heart and hand ;
That their aspects so friendly were,
That I should so my good will bear ;
To you, that are the worthiest,
The fairest and the gentleëst ;
And best can say, and best can do
That 'longs, methinks, a woman to ;
And therefore are most worthy far,
To be beloved as you are.
And so says Hope in all his tale,
Whereby he easeth all my bale.
For I believe, and think it true
That he doth speak or say of you.
And thus contented, lo ! I stand
With that, that Hope bears me in hand,
That you are mine, and shall so be.
Which Hope I keep full sure in me,

As he, that all my comfort is.
On you alone, which are my bliss,
My pleasure chief, which most I find,
And e'en the whole joy of my mind :
And shall so be, until the death
Shall make me yield up life and breath.
Thus, good mine own, lo ! here my trust ;
Lo ! here my truth, and service just ;
Lo ! in what case for you I stand !
Lo ! how you have me in your hand ;
And if you can requite a man,
Requite me, as you find me than.

ECCLESIASTES.

CHAPTER I.

SOLOMON, David's son, King of
          Jerusalem,
        Chosen by God to teach the Jews, and
          in his laws to lead them,
Confess, under the Sun that every thing is vain ;
The world is false ; man he is frail, and all his
          pleasures pain.
Alas ! what stable fruit may Adam's children find
In that they seek by sweat of brows and travail of
          their mind !
We, that live on the earth, draw toward our decay;
Our children fill our place a while, and then they
          fade away.

Such changes make the earth, and doth remove for
　　none ;
But serves us for a place to play our tragedies upon.
When that the restless sun westward his course
　　hath run,
Towards the east he hastes as fast to rise where
　　he begun.
When hoary Boreas hath blown his frozen blast,
Then Zephyrus, with his gentle breath, dissolves
　　the ice as fast.
Floods that drink up small brooks, and swell by
　　rage of rain,
Discharge in seas ; which them repulse, and swal-
　　low straight again.
These worldly pleasures, Lord ! so swift they run
　　their race,
That scarce our eyes may them discern ; they bide
　　so little space.
What hath been but is now; the like hereafter shall:
What new device grounded so sure, that dreadeth
　　not the fall !
What may be called new, but such things in times
　　past
As Time buried, and doth revive ; and Time again
　　shall waste.
Things past right worthy fame, have now no bruit
　　at all ;
Even so shall die such things as now the simple
　　wonders call.
I, that in David's seat sit crowned, and rejoice,
That with my sceptre rule the Jews, and teach
　　them with my voice,
Have searched long to know all things under the sun ;

To see how in this mortal life a surety might be won.
This kindled will to know; strange things for to
    desire,
God hath graft in our greedy breasts a torment for
    our hire.
The end of each travail forthwith I sought to know ;
I found them vain, mixed with gall, and burthen'd
    with much woe.
Defaults of nature's work no man's hand may re-
    store,
Which be in number like the sands upon the salt
    floods shore.
Then, vaunting in my wit, I gan call to my mind
What rules of wisdom I had taught, that elders
    could not find.
And, as by contraries to try most things we use,
Men's follies, and their errors eke I gan them all
    peruse;
Thereby with more delight to knowledge for to
    climb :
But this I found an endless work of pain, and loss
    of time.
For he to wisdom's school that doth apply his mind,
The further that he wades therein, the greater
    doubts shall find.
And such as enterprise to put new things in ure,
Of some that shall scorn their device, may well
    themselves assure.

CHAPTER II.

FROM pensive fancies then I gan my heart
       revoke ;
And gave me to such sporting plays as
       laughter might provoke :
But even such vain delights, when they most blinded
    me,
Always, methought, with smiling grace a king did
    ill agree.
Then sought I how to please my belly with much
    wine,
To feed me fat with costly feasts of rare delights,
    and fine ;
And other pleasures eke to purchase me, with rest:
In so great choice to find the thing that might
    content me best.
But, Lord ! what care of mind, what sudden storms
    of ire,
What broken sleeps endured I, to compass my desire !
To build me houses fair then set I all my cure :
By princely acts thus strove I still to make my
    fame endure.
Delicious gardens eke I made to please my sight ;
And graft therein all kinds of fruits that might my
    mouth delight.
Conduits, by lively springs from their old course I
    drew,
For to refresh the fruitful trees that in my gardens
    grew.
Of cattle great increase I bred in little space ;

Bondmen I bought; I gave them wives, and serv'd
    me with their race.
Great heaps of shining gold by sparing gan I save;
With things of price so furnished as fits a prince
    to have.
To hear fair women sing sometime I did rejoice;
Ravished with their pleasant tunes, and sweetness
    of their voice.
Lemans I had, so fair and of so lively hue,
That whoso gazed in their face might well their
    beauty rue.
Never erst sat there king so rich in David's seat;
Yet still, methought, for so small gain the travail
    was too great.
From my desirous eyes I hid no pleasant sight,
Nor from my heart no kind of mirth that might
    give them delight:
Which was the only fruit I reap'd of all my pain,
To feed my eyes, and to rejoice my heart with all
    my gain.
But when I made my count, with how great care
    of mind
And hearts unrest, that I had sought so wasteful
    fruit to find;
Then was I striken straight with that abused fire,
To glory in that goodly wit that compass'd my
    desire.
But fresh before mine eyes grace did my faults
    renew:
What gentle callings I had fled my ruin to pursue;
What raging pleasures past, peril and hard escape;
What fancies in my head had wrought the liquor
    of the grape.

The error then I saw that their frail hearts doth
    move,
Which strive in vain for to compare with Him that
    sits above :
In whose most perfect works such craft appeareth
    plain,
That to the least of them, there may no mortal
    hand attain.
And like as lightsome day doth shine above the
    night,
So dark to me did folly seem, and wisdom's beams
    as bright,
Whose eyes did seem so clear motes to discern and
    find :
But Will had closed Folly's eyes, which groped
    like the blind,
Yet death and time consume all wit and worldly
    fame ;
And look ! what end that folly hath, and wisdom
    hath the same.
Then said I thus : ' O Lord ! may not thy wisdom
    cure
The wailful wrongs and hard conflicts that folly
    doth endure ?'
To sharp my wit so fine then why took I this pain ?
Now find I well this noble search may eke be
    called vain.
As slander's loathsome bruit sounds folly's just
    reward,
Is put to silence all betime, and brought in small
    regard :
Even so doth time devour the noble blast of fame,
Which should resound their glories great that do
    deserve the same.

Thus present changes chase away the wonders past,
Ne is the wise man's fatal thread yet longer spun
    to last.
Then in this wretched vale, our life I loathed plain,
When I beheld our fruitless pains to compass
    pleasures vain.
My travail this avail hath me produced, lo !
An heir unknown shall reap the fruit that I in seed
    did sow.
But whereunto the Lord his nature shall incline
Who can foreknow, into whose hands I must my
    goods resign ?
But, Lord, how pleasant sweet then seem'd the
    idle life,
That never charged was with care, nor burthened
    with strife.
And vile the greedy trade of them that toil so sore,
To leave to such their travails fruit that never
    sweat therefore.
What is that pleasant gain ? what is that sweet re-
    lief,
That should delay the bitter taste that we feel of
    our grief?
The gladsome days we pass to search a simple gain ;
The quiet nights, with broken sleeps, to feed a
    restless brain.
What hope is left us then ?   What comfort doth
    remain
Our quiet hearts for to rejoice with the fruit of our
    pain ?
If that be true, who may himself so happy call
As I whose free and sumptuous spence doth shine
    beyond them all ?

Surely it is a gift and favour of the Lord,
Liberally to spend our goods, the ground of all
    discord.
And wretched hearts have they that let their trea-
    sures mould,
And carry the rod that scourgeth them that glory
    in their gold.
But I do know, by proof, whose riches bear such
    bruit,
What stable wealth may stand in waste, or heaping
    of such fruit.

CHAPTER III.

IKE to the steerless boat that swerves with
    every wind,
    The slipper top of worldly wealth, by cruel
    proof I find.
Scarce hath the seed, whereof that nature form-
    eth man,
Received life, when death him yields to earth
    where he began !
The grafted plants with pain, whereof we hoped
    fruit,
To root them up, with blossoms spread, then is
    our chief pursuit.
That erst we reared up, we undermine again ;
And shred the sprays whose growth sometime we
    laboured with pain.
Each froward threat'ning chere of fortune makes us
    plain ;

And every pleasant show revives our woful hearts
  again.
Ancient walls to rase is our unstable guise ;
And of their weather-beaten stones, to build some
  new device.
New fancies daily spring, which vade,[1] returning
  mo';
And now we practise to obtain that straight we
  must forego.
Some time we seek to spare that afterward we
  waste ;
And that we travail'd sore to knit, for to unloose
  as fast.
In sober silence now our quiet lips we close ;
And with unbridled tongues forthwith our secret
  hearts disclose.
Such as in folded arms we did embrace, we hate ;
Whom straight we reconcile again, and banish all
  debate.
My seed, with labour sown, such fruit produceth
  me,
To waste my life in contraries that never shall agree.
From God these heavy cares are sent for our un-
  rests ;
And with such burdens for our wealth he fraughteth
  full our breasts.
All that the Lord hath wrought, hath beauty and
  good grace ;
And to each thing assigned is the proper time and
  place.
And granted eke to man of all the world's estate,

---

[1] Pass away.

And of each thing wrought in the same, to argue
    and debate.
Which art, though it approach the heavenly know-
    ledge most,
To search the natural ground of things,—yet all is
    labour lost.
But then the wandering eyes that long for surety
    sought,
Found that by pain no certain wealth might in
    this world be bought.
Who liveth in delight and seeks no greedy thrift,
But freely spends his goods, may think it is a
    secret gift.
Fulfilled shall it be what so the Lord intend;
Which no device of man's wit may advance, nor
    yet defend;
Who made all things of nought, that Adam's chil-
    dren might
Learn how to dread the Lord, that wrought such
    wonders in their sight.
The grisly wonders past, which time wears out of
    mind,
To be renewed in our days the Lord hath so as-
    sign'd.
Lo! thus his careful scourge doth steal on us un-
    ware;
Which, when the flesh hath clean forgot, he doth
    again repair.
When I in this vain search had wander'd sore my
    wit,
I saw a royal throne eke where as Justice should
    have sit.
Instead of whom I saw, with fierce and cruel mood,

Where wrong was set ; that bloody beast that
    drank the guiltless blood :
Then thought I thus : ' One day the Lord shall sit
    in doom,
To view his flock, and choose the pure ; the spotted
    have no room.'
Yet be such scourges sent, that each aggrieved
    mind
Like the brute beasts that swell in rage and fury
    by their kind,
His error may confess when he hath wrestled long ;
And then with patience may him arm : the sure
    defence of wrong.
For death, that of the beast the carrion doth de-
    vour,
Unto the noble kind of man presents the fatal hour.
The perfect form that God hath given to either
    man,
Or other beast, dissolve it shall to earth, where it
    began.
And who can tell if that the soul of man ascend ;
Or with the body if it die, and to the ground de-
    scend.
Wherefore each greedy heart that riches seeks to
    gain,
Gather may he that savoury fruit that springeth of
    his pain.
A mean convenient wealth I mean to take in worth ;
And with a hand of largess eke in measure pour it
    forth.
For treasure spent in life the body doth sustain ;
The heir shall waste the hoarded gold, amassed
    with much pain.

Nor may foresight of man such order give in life,
For to foreknow who shall rejoice[1] their gotten
      good with strife.

Chapter IV.

WHEN I bethought me well, under the rest-
            less Sun
      By folk of power what cruel works un-
            chastised were done ;
I saw where stood a herd by power of such opprest,
Out of whose eyes ran floods of tears, that bayned[2]
      all their breast ;
Devoid of comfort clean, in terror and distress ;
In whose defence none would arise such rigour to
      repress.
Then thought I thus : 'O Lord ! the dead, whose
      fatal hour
Is clean run out, more happy are ; whom that the
      worms devour :
And happiest is the seed that never did conceive ;
That never felt the wailful wrongs that mortal folk
      receive.'
And then I saw that wealth, and every honest gain
By travail won, and sweat of brows, gan grow into
      disdain,
Through sloth of careless folk, whom ease so fat
      doth feed ;
Whose idle hands do nought but waste the fruit of
      other's seed.

----

[1] Enjoy.   [2] Bathed.

Which to themselves persuade—that little got with
    ease
More thankful is, than kingdoms won by travail
    and disease.
Another sort I saw without both friend or kin,
Whose greedy ways yet never sought a faithful
    friend to win.
Whose wretched corpse no toil yet ever weary could;
Nor glutted ever were their eyes with heaps of
    shining gold.
But, if it might appear to their abused eyen,
To whose avail they travail so, and for whose sake
    they pine;
Then should they see what cause they have for to
    repent
The fruitless pains and eke the time that they in
    vain have spent.
Then gan I thus resolve—'More pleasant is the life
Of faithful friends that spend their goods in com-
    mon, without strife.'
For as the tender friend appeaseth every grief,
So, if he fall that lives alone, who shall be his
    relief?
The friendly feeres[1] lie warm in arms embraced
    fast;
Who sleeps alone, at every turn doth feel the
    winter blast:
What can he do but yield, that must resist alone?
If there be twain, one may defend the t'other over-
    thrown.
The single twined cords may no such stress endure

---

[1] Companions.

As cables braided threefold may, together wreathed
    sure.
In better far estate stand children, poor and wise,
Than aged kings, wedded to will, that work with-
    out advice.
In prison have I seen, or this, a woful wight
That never knew what freedom meant, nor tasted
    of delight;
With such unhoped hap in most despair hath met,
Within the hands that erst wore gyves[1] to have a
    sceptre set.
And by conjures[2] the seed of kings is thrust from
    state,
Whereon a grieved people work ofttimes their hid-
    den hate.
Other, without respect, I saw a friend or foe
With feet worn bare in tracing such,[3] whereas the
    honours grew.
And at death of a prince great routs revived strange,
Which fain their old yoke to discharge, rejoiced in
    the change.
But when I thought, to these as heavy even or
    more
Shall be the burden of his reign, as his that went
    before;
And that a train like great upon the dead attend,[4]
I gan conclude, each greedy gain hath its uncer-
    tain end.
In humble spirit is set the temple of the Lord;
Where if thou enter, look thy mouth and conscience
    may accord!

[1] Fetters.
[2] Conspiracies.
[3] Or, paths.
[4] Depend, MS.

Whose Church is built of love, and deckt with hot
    desire,
And simple faith; the yolden ghost[1] his mercy doth
    require.
Where perfectly for aye he in his word doth rest;
With gentle ear to hear thy suit, and grant thee
    thy request.
In boast of outward works he taketh no delight,
Nor waste of words; such sacrifice unsavoureth in
    his sight.

CHAPTER V.

WHEN that repentant tears hath cleansed
        clear from ill
        The charged breast; and grace hath
            wrought therein amending will;
With bold demands then may his mercy well assail
The speech man saith, without the which request
    may none prevail.
More shall thy penitent sighs his endless mercy
    please,
Than their importune suits, which dream that words
    God's wrath appease.
For heart, contrite of fault, is gladsome recom-
    pense;
And prayer, fruit of Faith, whereby God doth with
    sin dispense.
As fearful broken sleeps spring from a restless head,

───────────────

[1] That is, the spirit yielded up to his will.

By chattering of unholy lips is fruitless prayer bred.
In waste of wind, I rede,[1] vow nought unto the Lord,
Whereto thy heart to bind thy will, freely doth not
    accord ;
For humble vows fulfill'd, by grace right sweetly
    smoke :
But bold behests, broken by lusts, the wrath of
    God provoke.
Yet bet[2] with humble heart thy frailty to confess,
Than to boast of such perfectness, whose works
    such fraud express.
With feigned words and oaths contract with God
    no guile ;
Such craft returns to thine own harm, and doth
    thyself defile.
And though the mist of sin persuade such error
    light,
Thereby yet are thy outward works all dampned[3]
    in his sight.
As sundry broken dreams us diversly abuse,
So are his errors manifold that many words doth
    use.
With humble secret plaint, few words of hot effect,
Honour thy Lord ; allowance vain of void desert
    neglect.
Though wrong at times the right, and wealth eke
    need oppress,
Think not the hand of justice slow to follow the
    redress.
For such unrighteous folk as rule withouten dread,
By some abuse or secret lust he suffereth to be led.
The chief bliss that in earth to living man is lent,

[1] I advise.   [2] Better.   [3] Condemned.

Is moderate wealth to nourish life, if he can be
  content.
He that hath but one field, and greedily seeketh
  nought,
To fence the tiller's hand from need, is king within
  his thought.
But such as of their gold their only idol make,
No treasure may the raven of their hungry hands
  aslake.
For he that gapes for good, and hoardeth all his gain,
Travails in vain to hide the sweet that should re-
  lieve his pain.
Where is great wealth, there should be many a
  needy wight
To spend the same; and that should be the rich
  man's chief delight.
The sweet and quiet sleeps that wearied limbs op-
  press,
Beguile the night in diet thin, not feasts of great
  excess :
But waker[1] lie the rich; whose lively heat with rest
Their charged bulks[2] with change of meats cannot
  so soon digest.
Another righteous doom I saw of greedy gain ;
With busy cares such treasures oft preserved to
  their bane :
The plenteous houses sackt; the owners end with
  shame
Their sparkled goods ; their needy heirs, that should
  enjoy the same,
From wealth despoiled bare, from whence th y
  came they went ;

[1] Wakeful.   [2] Bodies.

Clad in the clothes of poverty, as Nature first them
    sent.
Naked as from the womb we came, if we depart,
With toil to seek that we must leave, what boot
    to vex the heart?
What life lead testy men then, that consume their
    days
In inward frets, untemper'd hates, at strife with
    some always.
Then gan I praise all those, in such a world of
    strife,
As take the profit of their goods, that may be had
    in life.
For sure the liberal hand that hath no heart to spare
This fading wealth, but pours it forth, it is a virtue
    rare:
That makes wealth slave to need, and gold become
    his thrall,
Clings[1] not his guts with niggish[2] fare, to heap
    his chest withal;
But feeds the lusts of kind with costly meats and
    wine;
And slacks the hunger and the thirst of needy folk
    that pine.
No glutton's feast I mean in waste of spence[3] to
    strive;
But temperate meals the dulled spirits with joy
    thus to revive.
No care may pierce where mirth hath temper'd
    such a breast:
The bitter gall, season'd with sweet, such wisdom
    may digest.

   [1] Starve.   [2] Niggard.   [3] Expense.

H

CERTAIN PSALMS.

The Prologue.

HERE rechless[1] youth in an unquiet
    breast,
  Set on by wrath, revenge, and cruelty,
  After long war patience had oppress'd ;
And justice, wrought by princely equity ;
My Denny[2] then, mine error deep imprest,
Began to work despair of liberty ;
Had not David, the perfect warrior taught,
That of my fault thus pardon should be sought.

Domine Deus salutis. Psalm LXXXVIII.

LORD ! upon whose will dependeth my
    welfare,
  To call upon thy holy name, since day nor
    night I spare,
Grant that the just request of this repentant mind
So pierce thine ears, that in thy sight some favour
   it may find.

---

[1] Careless.
[2] In the old edition the name does not occur, and the word 'conscience' is substituted. Dr. Nott suggests that this person was "Sir Walter Denny, an intimate friend of the Howard family, and afterwards one of the executors of Henry the Eighth's will."

My soul is fraughted full with grief of follies past;
My restless body doth consume, and death ap-
    proacheth fast:
Like them, whose fatal thread thy hand hath cut
    in twain;
Of whom there is no further bruit, which in their
    graves remain.
O Lord! thou hast me cast headlong, to please my
    foe,
Into a pit all bottomless, where, as I plain[1] my
    woe,
The burden of thy wrath it doth me sore oppress;
And sundry storms thou hast me sent of terror and
    distress.
The faithful friends are fled and banished from my
    sight:
And such as I have held full dear, have set my
    friendship light.
My durance doth persuade of freedom such despair,
That by the tears that bain my breast, mine eye-
    sight doth appair.[2]
Yet do I never cease thine aid for to desire,
With humble heart and stretched hands, for to
    appease thine ire.
Wherefore dost thou forbear in the defence of thine,
To shew such tokens of thy power in sight of
    Adam's line;
Whereby each feeble heart with faith might so be
    fed,
That in the mouth of thy elect thy mercies might
    be spread.

[1] Mourn.   [2] Fail, impair.

The flesh that feedeth worms cannot thy love de-
    clare !
Nor such set forth thy praise as dwell in the land
    of despair.
In blind indured hearts light of thy lively name
Cannot appear, nor cannot judge the brightness of
    the same.
Nor blazed may thy name be by the mouths of
    those
Whom death hath shut in silence, so as they may
    not disclose.
The lively voice of them that in thy word delight,
Must be the trump that must resound the glory of
    thy might.
Wherefore I shall not cease, in chief of my distress
To call on Thee, till that the sleep my wearied
    limbs oppress.
And in the morning eke, when that the sleep is
    fled,
With floods of salt repentant tears to wash my
    restless bed.
Within this careful mind, burden'd with care and
    grief,
Why dost thou not appear, O Lord ! that shouldst
    be his relief?
My wretched state behold, whom death shall straight
    assail ;
Of one, from youth afflicted still, that never did
    but wail.
The dread, lo ! of thine ire hath trod me under
    feet :
The scourges of thine angry hand hath made death
    seem full sweet.

Like as the roaring waves the sunken ship sur-
　　round,
Great heaps of care did swallow me, and I no
　　succour found:
For they whom no mischance could from my love
　　divide,
Are forced, for my greater grief, from me their
　　face to hide.

THE PROLOGUE.

HE sudden storms that heave me to and
　　fro,
　　Had well near pierced Faith, my guiding
　　sail;
For I, that on the noble voyage go
To succour truth, and falsehood to assail,
Constrained am to bear my sails full low;
And never could attain some pleasant gale.
For unto such the prosperous winds do blow
As run from port to port to seek avail.[1]
This bred despair; whereof such doubts did grow
That I gan faint, and all my courage fail.
But now, my BLAGE,[2] mine error well I see;
Such goodly light king David giveth me.

[1] Advantage.
[2] "Blame" in the old edition.   George Blage, a friend of
Surrey's, who accompanied him to Landrecy.   He was of a
good Kentish family, was educated at Cambridge, and addressed a poem to Lord Wriothesley.

Quam bonus Israel Deus. PSALM LXXIII.

THOUGH, Lord, to Israel thy graces plen-
teous be;
I mean to such, with pure intent as fix
their trust in Thee,
Yet whiles the Faith did faint that should have
been my guide,
Like them that walk in slipper paths, my feet be-
gan to slide;
Whiles I did grudge at those that glory in their
gold,
Whose loathsome pride enjoyeth wealth in quiet,
as they would.
To see by course of years what nature doth appair.[1]
The palaces of princely form succeed from heir to
heir.
From all such travails free, as 'long to Adam's
seed,
Neither withdrawn from wicked works by danger,
nor by dread.
Whereof their scornful pride, and gloried with their
eyes;
As garments clothe the naked man, thus are they
clad in vice.
Thus, as they wish, succeeds the mischief that they
mean;
Whose glutted cheeks sloth feeds so fat, as scant
their eyes be seen.[2]

---

[1] Impair, or bring to decay.
[2] This seems aimed at King Henry VIII.

Unto whose cruel power most men for dread are
    fain
To bend or bow; with lofty looks, whiles they
    vaunt in their reign;
And in their bloody hands, whose cruelty that
    frame
The wailful works that scourge the poor, without
    regard of blame.
To tempt the living God they think it no offence;
And pierce the simple with their tongues that can
    make no defence.
Such proofs before the just, to cause the hearts to
    waver,
Be set like cups mingled with gall, of bitter taste
    and savour.
Then say thy foes in scorn, that taste no other food,
But suck the flesh of thy Elect, and bathe them in
    their blood;
' Should we believe the Lord doth know, and suf-
    fer this?
Fooled be he with fables vain that so abused is.'
In terror of the just, that reigns iniquity,
Armed with power, laden with gold, and dread for
    cruelty.
Then vain the war might seem, that I by faith
    maintain
Against the flesh, whose false effects my pure
    heart would disdain.
For I am scourged still, that no offence have done,
By wrathès children; and from my birth my chas-
    tising begun.
When I beheld their pride, and slackness of thy
    hand,

I gan bewail the woful state wherein thy chosen
    stand.
And when I sought whereof thy sufferance, Lord,
    should grow,
I found no wit could pierce so far, thy holy dooms
    to know :
And that no mysteries, nor doubt could be distrust,
Till I come to the holy place, the mansion of the
    just ;
Where I shall see what end thy justice shall pre-
    pare,
For such as build on worldly wealth, and dye their
    colours fair.
Oh ! how their ground is false ! and all their
    building vain !
And they shall fall ; their power shall fail that did
    their pride maintain.
As charged hearts with care, that dream some plea-
    sant turn,
After their sleep find their abuse, and to their
    plaint return ;
So shall their glory fade ; thy sword of vengeance
    shall
Unto their drunken eyes in blood disclose their
    errors all.
And when their golden fleece is from their back
    y-shorn ;
The spots that underneath were hid, thy chosen
    sheep shall scorn :
And till that happy day, my heart shall swell in
    care,
My eyes yield tears, my years consume between
    hope and despair.

Lo! how my spirits are dull, and all thy judgments
    dark,
No mortal head may scale so high, but wonder at
    thy work.
Alas! how oft my foes have framed my decay;
But when I stood in dread to drench,[1] thy hands
    still did me stay.
And in each voyage that I took to conquer sin,
Thou wert my guide, and gave me grace, to com-
    fort me therein.
And when my wither'd skin unto my bones did
    cleave,
And flesh did waste, thy grace did then my simple
    spirits relieve.
In other succour then, O Lord! why should I
    trust;
But only thine, whom I have found in thy behight[2]
    so just.
And such for dread, or gain as shall thy name re-
    fuse,
Shall perish with their golden gods that did their
    hearts seduce.
While[3] I, that in thy word have set my trust and
    joy,
The high reward that 'longs thereto shall quietly
    enjoy.
And my unworthy lips, inspired with thy grace,
Shall thus forespeak thy secret works, in sight of
    Adam's race.

---

[1] To be overwhelmed.   [2] Promise.   [3] MS. Where.

Exaudi, Deus, orationem meam.   PSALM LV.

GIVE ear to my suit, Lord ! fromward[1] hide
          not thy face :
     Behold ! hearken, in grief, lamenting how
          I pray :
My foes that bray so loud, and eke threpe on[2] so
          fast,
Buckled to do me scath,[3] so is their malice bent.
Care pierceth my entrails, and travaileth my spirit ;
The grisly fear of death environeth my breast :
A trembling cold of dread overwhelmeth my heart.
' Oh !' think I, ' had I wings like to the simple
          dove,
This peril might I fly ; and seek some place of rest
In wilder woods, where I might dwell far from
          these cares.'
What speedy way of wing my plaints should they
          lay on,
To 'scape the stormy blast that threaten'd is to me ?
Rein those unbridled tongues ! break that conjured
          league !
For I decipher'd have amid our town the strife.
Guile and wrong keep the walls ; they ward both
          day and night :
And mischief join'd with care doth keep the market-
          stead :
Whilst wickedness with crafts in heaps swarm
          through the street.

----

[1] Away from.   [2] To accuse with clamour.   [3] Injury.

Ne my declared foe wrought me all this reproach.
By harm so looked for, it weigheth half the less.
For though mine enemies hap had been for to
      prevail,
I could have hid my face from venom of his eye.
It was a friendly foe, by shadow of good will ;
Mine old fere,[1] and dear friend, my guide that
      trapped me ;
Where I was wont to fetch the cure of all my care,
And in his bosom hide my secret zeal to God.
With such sudden surprise, quick may him hell
      devour ;
Whilst I invoke the Lord, whose power shall me
      defend,
My prayer shall not cease, from that the sun des-
      cends,
Till he his alture[2] win, and hide them in the sea,
With words of hot effect,[3] that moveth from heart
      contrite,
Such humble suit, O Lord, doth pierce thy patient
      ear.
It was the Lord that brake the bloody compacts of
      those
That pricked on with ire, to slaughter me and mine.
The everlasting God, whose kingdom hath no end,
Whom by no tale to dread he could divert from sin,
The conscience unquiet he strikes with heavy hand,
And proves their force in faith, whom he sware
      to defend.
Butter falls not so soft as doth his patience long,
And overpasseth fine oil running not half so
      smooth.

[1] Companion.   [2] Altitude.   [3] Affection; passion.

But when his sufferance finds that bridled wrath
    provokes,
His threatened wrath he whets more sharp than
    tool can file.
Friar! whose harm and tongue presents the wicked
    sort,
Of those false wolves, with coats which do their
    ravin hide;
That swear to me by heaven, the footstool of the
    Lord,
Though force had hurt my fame, they did not touch
    my life.
Such patching care I loath, as feeds the wealth
    with lies;
But in the other Psalm of David find I ease.[1]
Jacta curam tuam super Dominum ; et ipse te enutriet.

Domine, Dominus noster.   PSALM VIII.

THY name, O Lord, how great, is found be-
    fore our sight!
    It fills the earth, and spreads the air: the
    great works of thy might!
For even unto the heavens thy power hath given a
    place,
And closed it above their heads; a mighty, large,
    compass.

---

[1] This may refer to some other Psalm which was to have
followed.

Thy praise what cloud can hide, but it will shine
      again :
Since young and tender sucking babes have power
      to shew it plain.
Which in despight of those that would thy glory
      hide,
[Thou] hast put into such infants' mouths for to
      confound their pride.
Wherefore I shall behold thy figur'd heaven so high,
Which shews such prints of divers forms within the
      cloudy sky :
As hills, and shapes of men ; eke beasts of sundry
      kind,
Monstrous to our outward sight, and fancies of our
      mind.
And eke the wanish moon, which sheens by night
      also ;
And each one of the wandering stars, which after
      her do go.
And how these keep their course ; and which are
      those that stands ;
Because they be thy wondrous works, and labours
      of thy hands.
But yet among all these I ask, ' What thing is man ?'
Whose turn to serve in his poor need this work
      Thou first began.
Or what is Adam's son that bears his father's mark ?
For whose delight and comfort eke Thou hast
      wrought all this work.
I see thou mind'st him much, that dost reward
      him so :
Being but earth, to rule the earth, whereon him-
      self doth go.

From angel's substance eke Thou mad'st him differ
    small;
Save one doth change his life awhile; the other
    not at all.
The sun and moon also Thou mad'st to give him
    light;
And each one of the wandering stars to twinkle
    sparkles bright.
The air to give him breath; the water for his
    health;
The earth to bring forth grain and fruit, for to in-
    crease his wealth.
And many metals too, for pleasure of the eye;
Which in the hollow sounded ground in privy veins
    do lie.
The sheep to give his wool, to wrap his body in;
And for such other needful things, the ox to spare
    his skin.
The horse even at his will to bear him to and fro;
And as him list each other beast to serve his turn also.
The fishes of the sea likewise to feed him oft;
And eke the birds, whose feathers serve to make
    his sides lie soft.
On whose head thou hast set a crown of glory too,
To whom also thou didst appoint, that honour
    should be do.
And thus thou mad'st him lord of all this work of
    thine;
Of man that goes, of beast that creeps, whose looks
    doth down decline;
Of fish that swim below, of fowls that fly on high,
Of sea that finds the air his rain, and of the land
    so dry.

And underneath his feet, Thou hast set all this
  same ;
To make him know, and plain confess, that mar-
  vellous is thy name.
And, Lord, which art our Lord, how marvellous it
  is found
The heavens do shew, the earth doth tell, and eke
  the world so round.
Glory, therefore, be given to Thee first, which art
  Three ;
And yet but One Almighty God, in substance and
  degree :
As first it was when Thou the dark confused heap, ·
Clotted in one, didst part in four ; which elements
  we clepe :[1]
And as the same is now, even here within our time ;
So[2] ever shall hereafter be, when we be filth and
  slime.

---

[1] We call.   [2] MS. And.

THE SECOND BOOK OF VIRGIL'S ÆNEID.[1]

THEY whisted[2] all, with fixed face attent,
When prince Æneas from the royal seat
Thus gan to speak.   O Queen! it is
     thy will
I should renew a woe cannot be told:
How that the Greeks did spoil, and overthrow
The Phrygian wealth, and wailful realm of Troy:
Those ruthful things that I myself beheld;
And whereof no small part fell to my share.
Which to express, who could refrain from tears?
What Myrmidon? or yet what Dolopes?
What stern Ulysses' waged soldier?
And lo! moist night now from the welkin[3] falls;
And stars declining counsel us to rest.
But since so great is thy delight to hear
Of our mishaps, and Troyè's last decay;
Though to record the same my mind abhors,
And plaint eschews, yet thus will I begin.
     The Greeks' chieftains all irked[4] with the war
Wherein they wasted had so many years,

---

[1] The first edition is entitled "Certain Bokes of Virgiles
Aenæis turned into English meter by the right honorable
lorde, Henry Earle of Surrey. Apud Ricardum Tottel. Cum
priuilegio ad imprimendum solum, 1557." At the end,
" Imprinted at London in flete strete within Temple barre,
at the sygne of the hand and starre, by Richard Tottell the
xxi. day of June, An. 1557." 12mo.
     [2] Were silent.   [3] The sky.   [4] Wearied.

And oft repuls'd by fatal destiny,
A huge horse made, high raised like a hill,
By the divine science of Minerva:
Of cloven fir[1] compacted were his ribs ;
For their return a feigned sacrifice :
The fame whereof so wander'd it at point.
In the dark bulk they clos'd bodies of men
Chosen by lot, and did enstuff by stealth
The hollow womb with armed soldiers.

 There stands in sight an isle, hight Tenedon,
Rich, and of fame, while Priam's kingdom stood;
Now but a bay, and road, unsure for ship.
Hither them secretly the Greeks withdrew,
Shrouding themselves under the desert shore.
And, weening[2] we they had been fled and gone,
And with that wind had fet the land of Greece,
Troy discharged her long continued dole.
The gates cast up, we issued out to play,
The Greekish camp desirous to behold,
The places void, and the forsaken coasts.
'.Here Pyrrhus' band ; there fierce Achilles pight ;
Here rode their ships ; there did their battles join.'
Astonnied some the scatheful gift beheld,
Behight by vow unto the chaste Minerve ;
All wond'ring at the hugeness of the horse.

 And first of all Timœtes gan advise
Within the walls to lead and draw the same;
And place it eke amid the palace court :
Whether of guile, or Troyè's fate it would.
Capys, with some of judgment more discreet,
Will'd it to drown ; or underset with flame

---

[1] Wood easily set on fire.　　[2] Supposing.

1

The suspect present of the Greeks' deceit ;
Or bore and gage the hollow caves uncouth.
So diverse ran the giddy people's mind.
   Lo ! foremost of a rout that follow'd him,
Kindled Laocoon hasted from the tower,
Crying far off : ' O wretched citizens !
What so great kind of frenzy fretteth you ?
Deem ye the Greeks our enemies to be gone ?
Or any Greekish gifts can you suppose
Devoid of guile ? Is so Ulysses known ?
Either the Greeks are in this timber hid ;
Or this an engine is to annoy our walls,
To view our towers, and overwhelm our town.
Here lurks some craft. Good Troyans! give no trust
Unto this horse ; for what so ever it be,
I dread the Greeks ; yea ! when they offer gifts.'
And with that word, with all his force a dart
He lanced then into that crooked womb ;
Which trembling stack, and shook within the side :
Wherewith the caves gan hollowly resound.
And, but for Fates, and for our blind forecast,
The Greeks' device and guile had he descried ;
Troy yet had stand, and Priam's towers so high.
   Therewith behold, whereas the Phrygian herds
Brought to the king with clamour, all unknown
A young man, bound his hands behind his back ;
Who willingly had yielden prisoner,
To frame his guile, and open Troyè's gates
Unto the Greeks ; with courage fully bent,
And mind determed either of the twain ;
To work his feat, or willing yield to death.
Near him, to gaze, the Trojan youth gan flock,
And strave who most might at the captive scorn.

The Greeks' deceit behold, and by one proof
Imagine all the rest.
   For in the press as he unarmed stood
With troubled cheer, and Phrygian routs beset;
'Alas!' quod he, 'what earth now, or what seas
May me receive? Catiff, what rests me now?
For whom in Greece doth no abode remain.
The Trojans eke offended seek to wreak
Their heinous wrath, with shedding of my blood.'
   With this regret our hearts from rancour moved.
The bruit appeas'd, we ask'd him of his birth,
What news he brought; what hope made him to
       yield.
   Then he, all dread removed, thus began:
'O King! I shall, what ever me betide,
Say but the truth: ne first will me deny
A Grecian born; for though fortune hath made
Sinon a wretch, she cannot make him false.
If ever came unto your ears the name,
Nobled by fame, of the sage Palamede,
Whom trait'rously the Greeks condemn'd to die;
Guiltless, by wrongful doom, for that he did
Dissuade the wars; whose death they now lament;
Underneath him my father, bare of wealth,
Into his band young, and near of his blood,
In my prime years unto the war me sent.
While that by fate his state in stay did stand,
And when his realm did flourish by advice,
Of glory, then, we bare some fame and bruit.
But since his death by false Ulysses' sleight,
(I speak of things to all men well beknown)
A dreary life in doleful plaint I led,
Repining at my guiltless friend's mischance.

Ne could I, fool! refrain my tongue from threats,
That if my chance were ever to return
Victor to Arge, to follow my revenge.
With such sharp words procured I great hate.
Here sprang my harm. Ulysses ever sith
With new found crimes began me to affray.
In common ears false rumours gan he sow:
Weapons of wreak his guilty mind gan seek.
Ne rested aye till he by Calchas mean ———
But whereunto these thankless tales in vain
Do I rehearse, and linger forth the time,
In like estate if all the Greeks ye price?
It is enough ye here rid me at once.
Ulysses, Lord! how he would this rejoice!
Yea, and either Atride would bye[1] it dear.'

    This kindled us more eager to inquire,
And to demand the cause; without suspect
Of so great mischief thereby to ensue,
Or of Greeks' craft. He then with forged words
And quivering limbs, thus took his tale again.
    'The Greeks ofttimes intended their return
From Troyè town, with long wars all ytired,
For to dislodge; which, would God! they had done.
But oft the winter storms of raging seas,
And oft the boisterous winds did them to stay;
And chiefly, when of clinched ribs of fir
This horse was made, the storms roared in the air.
Then we in doubt to Phœbus' temple sent
Euripilus, to weet[2] the prophesy.
From whence he brought these woful news again.
With blood, O Greeks! and slaughter of a maid,

---

[1] Abide, or suffer.   [2] To learn.

Ye peas'd the winds, when first ye came to Troy.
With blood likewise ye must seek your return :
A Greekish soul must offer'd be therefore.'
  ' But when this sound had pierc'd the peoples'
    ears,
With sudden fear astonied were their minds ;
The chilling cold did overrun their bones,
To whom that fate was shap'd, whom Phœbus
    would.'
Ulysses then amid the press brings in
Calchas with noise, and will'd him to discuss
The Gods' intent.   Then some gan deem to me
The cruel wreak of him that fram'd the craft ;
Foreseeing secretly what would ensue.
In silence then, yshrowding him from sight,
But days twice five he whisted ; and refused
To death, by speech, to further any wight.
At last, as forced by false Ulysses' cry,
Of purpose he brake forth, assigning me
To the altar ; whereto they granted all :
And that, that erst each one dread to himself,
Returned all unto my wretched death.
And now at hand drew near the woful day.
All things prepar'd wherewith to offer me ;
Salt, corn, fillets, my temples for to bind.
I scap'd the death, I grant ! and brake the bands,
And lurked in a marish all the night
Among the ooze, while they did set their sails ;
If it so be that they indeed so did.
Now rests no hope my native land to see,
My children dear, nor long desired sire ;
On whom, perchance, they shall wreak my escape :
Those harmless wights shall for my fault be slain.

'Then, by the gods, to whom all truth is known;
By faith unfil'd, if any anywhere
With mortal folk remains ; I thee beseech,
O king, thereby rue on my travail great :
Pity a wretch that guiltless suffereth wrong.'
    Life to these tears with pardon eke, we grant.
And Priam first himself commands to loose
His gyves, his bands ; and friendly to him said :
'Whoso thou art, learn to forget the Greeks :
Henceforth be ours ; and answer me with truth :
Whereto was wrought the mass of this huge horse ?
Whose the devise ? and whereto should it tend ?
What holy vow ? or engine for the wars ?'
    Then he, instruct with wiles and Greekish craft,
His loosed hands lift upward to the stars :
'Ye everlasting lamps ! I testify,
Whose power divine may not be violate ;
Th' altar, and sword,' quoth he, 'that I have scap'd;
Ye sacred bands ! I wore as yielden host ;
Lawful be it for me to break mine oath
To Greeks ; lawful to hate their nation ;
Lawful be it to sparkle in the air
Their secrets all, whatso they keep in close :
For free am I from Greece and from their laws.
So be it, Troy, and saved by me from scathe,
Keep faith with me, and stand to thy behest ;
If I speak truth, and opening things of weight,
For grant of life requite thee large amends.
    'The Greeks' whole hope of undertaken war
In Pallas' help consisted evermore.
But sith the time that wicked Diomed,
Ulysses eke, that forger of all guile,
Adventur'd from the holy sacred fane

For to bereave Dame Pallas' fatal form,
And slew the watches of the chiefest tower,
And then away the holy statue stole;
(That were so bold with hands embrued in blood,
The virgin Goddess veils for to defile)
Sith that, their hope gan fail, their hope to fall,
Their pow'r appair, their Goddess' grace withdraw;
Which with no doubtful signs she did declare.
Scarce was the statue to our tents ybrought,
But she gan stare with sparkled eyes of flame;
Along her limbs the salt sweat trickled down:
Yea thrice herself, a hideous thing to tell!
In glances bright she glittered from the ground,
Holding in hand her targe and quivering spear.
Calchas by sea then bade us haste our flight:
Whose engines might not break the walls of Troy,
Unless at Greece they would renew their lots,
Restore the God that they by sea had brought
In warped keels.   To Arge sith they be come,
They 'pease their Gods, and war afresh prepare.
And cross the seas unlooked for eftsoons
They will return.   This order Calchas set.
    ' This figure made they for th' aggrieved God,
In Pallas' stead; to cleanse their heinous fault.
Which mass he willed to be reared high
Toward the skies, and ribbed all with oak,
So that your gates ne wall might it receive;
Ne yet your people might defensed be
By the good zeal of old devotion.
For if your hands did Pallas' gift defile,
To Priam's realm great mischief should befall:
Which fate the Gods first on himself return.
But had your own hands brought it in your town,

Asia should pass, and carry offer'd war
In Greece, e'en to the walls of Pelop's town;
And we and ours that destiny endure.'

By such like wiles of Sinon, the forsworn,
His tale with us did purchase credit; some,
Trapt by deceit; some, forced by his tears;
Whom neither Diomed, nor great Achille,
Nor ten years war, ne a thousand sail could daunt.

Us caitiffs then a far more dreadful chance
Befel, that troubled our unarmed breasts.
Whiles Laocoon, that chosen was by lot
Neptunus' priest, did sacrifice a bull
Before the holy altar; suddenly
From Tenedon, behold! in circles great
By the calm seas come fleeting adders twain,
Which plied towards the shore (I loathe to tell)
With reared breast lift up above the seas:
Whose bloody crests aloft the waves were seen;
The hinder part swam hidden in the flood.
Their grisly backs were linked manifold.
With sound of broken waves they gat the strand,
With glowing eyen, tainted with blood and fire;
Whose waltring tongues did lick their hissing
        mouths.
We fled away; our face the blood forsook:
But they with gait direct to Lacon ran.
And first of all each serpent doth enwrap
The bodies small of his two tender sons;
Whose wretched limbs they bit, and fed thereon.
Then raught they him, who had his weapon caught
To rescue them; twice winding him about,
With folded knots and circled tails, his waist:
Their scaled backs did compass twice his neck,

With reared heads aloft and stretched throats.
He with his hands strave to unloose the knots,
(Whose sacred fillets all-besprinkled were
With filth of gory blood, and venom rank)
And to the stars such dreadful shouts he sent,
Like to the sound the roaring bull forth lows,
Which from the halter wounded doth astart,
The swerving axe when he shakes from his neck.
The serpents twine, with hasted trail they glide
To Pallas' temple, and her towers of height :
Under the feet of which the Goddess stern,
Hidden behind her target's boss they crept.
New gripes of dread then pierce our trembling
        breasts.
They said ; Lacon's deserts had dearly bought
His heinous deed ; that pierced had with steel
The sacred bulk, and thrown the wicked lance.
The people cried with sundry greeing shouts
To bring the horse to Pallas' temple blive ;[1]
In hope thereby the Goddess' wrath t' appease.
We cleft the walls and closures of the town ;
Whereto all help : and underset the feet
With sliding rolls, and bound his neck with ropes.
This fatal gin thus overclamb our walls,
Stuft with arm'd men ; about the which there ran
Children and maids,[2] that holy carols sang ;
And well were they whose hands might touch the
        cords !
With threat'ning cheer thus slided through our
        town
The subtle tree, to Pallas' temple-ward.

---

[1] Immediately.   [2] That is, boys and girls.

O native land! Ilion! and of the gods
The mansion place!   O warlike walls of Troy!
Four times it stopt in th' entry of our gate;
Four times the harness[1] clatter'd in the womb.
But we go on, unsound of memory,
And blinded eke by rage persever still:
This fatal monster in the fane we place.

   Cassandra then, inspired with Phœbus sprite,
Her prophet's lips, yet never of us 'lieved,
Disclosed eft; forespeaking things to come.
We wretches, lo! that last day of our life
With boughs of fest[2] the town, and temples deck.

   With this the sky gan whirl about the sphere:
The cloudy night gan thicken from the sea,
With mantles spread that cloaked earth and skies,
And eke the treason of the Greekish guile.
The watchmen lay dispers'd to take their rest;
Whose wearied limbs sound sleep had then op-
       press'd:
When, well in order comes the Grecian fleet
From Tenedon, toward the coasts well known,
By friendly silence of the quiet moon.
When the king's ship put forth his mark of fire,
Sinon, preserved by froward destiny,
Let forth the Greeks enclosed in the womb:
The closures eke of pine by stealth unpinn'd,
Whereby the Greeks restored were to air.
With joy down hasting from the hollow tree,
With cords let down did slide unto the ground
The great captains; Sthenel, and Thessander,
And fierce Ulysses, Athamas, and Thoas;
Machaon first, and then king Menelae;

     [1] Arms, armour.   [2] Mirth.

Opeas eke that did the engine forge.
By cords let fall fast 'gan they slide adown,
And straight invade the town yburied then
With wine and sleep. And first the watch is slain:
Then gates unfold to let their fellows in,
They join themselves with the conjured bands.
   It was the time when granted from the Gods
The first sleep creeps most sweet in weary folk.
Lo! in my dream before mine eyes, methought,
With rueful cheer I saw where Hector stood,
(Out of whose eyes there gushed streams of tears)
Drawn at a car as he of late had be,
Distained with bloody dust, whose feet were bowln[1]
With the strait cords wherewith they haled him.
Ay me, what one? that Hector how unlike,
Which erst return'd clad with Achilles' spoils;
Or when he threw into the Greekish ships
The Trojan flame! so was his beard defiled,
His crisped locks all clust'red with his blood,
With all such wounds, as many he received
About the walls of that his native town.
Whom frankly thus, methought, I spake unto,
With bitter tears and doleful deadly voice:
' O Troyan light! O only hope of thine!
What lets so long thee staid? or from what coasts,
Our most desired Hector, dost thou come?
Whom, after slaughter of thy many friends,
And travail of the people, and thy town,
All-wearied lord! how gladly we behold!
What sorry chance hath stain'd thy lively face?
Or why see I these wounds, alas! so wide?'
He answer'd nought, nor in my vain demands

[1] Swollen.

Abode ; but from the bottom of his breast
Sighing he said : ' Flee, flee, O goddess' son !
And save thee from the fury of this flame.
Our en'mies now are masters of the walls ;
And Troyè town now falleth from the top.
Sufficeth that is done for Priam's reign.
If force might serve to succour Troyè town,
'This right hand well might have been her defence.
But Troyè now commendeth to thy charge
Her holy reliques, and her privy Gods.
Them join to thee, as fellows of thy fate.
Large walls rear thou for them : for so thou shalt,
After time spent in th' overwand'red flood.'
This said, he brought forth Vesta in his hands ;
Her fillets eke, and everlasting flame.

In this mean while with diverse plaint, the town
Throughout was spread ; and louder more and
      more
The din resounded : with rattling of arms,
Although mine old Father Anchises' house
Removed stood, with shadow hid of trees,
I waked : therewith to the house-top I clamb,
And hark'ning stood I : like as when the flame
Lights in the corn, by drift of boisterous wind ;
Or the swift stream that driveth from the hill,
Roots up the fields, and presseth the ripe corn,
And ploughed ground, and overwhelms the grove :
The silly herdman all astonnied stands,
From the high rock while he doth hear the sound.
    Then the Greeks' faith, then their deceit ap-
      peared.
Of Deiphobus the palace large and great
Fell to the ground, all overspread with flash.

His next neighbour Ucalegon afire:
The Sygean seas did glister all with flame.
Up sprang the cry of men, and trumpets blast.
Then, as distraught, I did my armour on;
Ne could I tell yet whereto arms avail'd.
But with our feres to throng out from the press
Toward the tower, our hearts brent with desire.
Wrath prick'd us forth; and unto us it seemed
A seemly thing to die arm'd in the field.
    Wherewith Panthus scap'd from the Greekish
        darts,
Otreus' son, Phœbus' priest, brought in hand
The sacred reliques, and the vanquish'd Gods:
And in his hand his little nephew led;
And thus, as phren'tic, to our gates he ran.
'Panthus,' quod I, 'in what estate stand we?
Or for refuge what fortress shall we take?'
Scarce spake I this, when wailing thus he said:
'The later day and fate of Troy is come;
The which no plaint or prayer may avail.
Troyans we were; and Troyè was sometime,
And of great fame the Teucrian glory erst:
Fierce Jove to Greece hath now transposed all.
The Greeks are lords over this fired town.
Yonder huge horse, that stands amid our walls,
Sheds armed men: and Sinon, victor now,
With scorn of us doth set all things on flame.
And, rushed in at our unfolded gates,
Are thousands mo' than ever came from Greece.
And some with weapons watch the narrow streets;
With bright swords drawn, to slaughter ready
        bent.
And scarce the watches of the gate began

Them to defend, and with blind fight resist.'
    Through Panthus' words, and lightning of the
        Gods,
Amid the flame and arms ran I in press,
As fury guided me, and whereas I had heard
The cry greatest that made the air resound.
Into our band then fell old Iphytus,
And Rypheus, that met us by moonlight;
Dymas and Hypanis joining to our side,
With young Chorebus, Mygdonius' son;
Which in those days at Troy did arrive,
(Burning with rage of dame Cassandra's love)
In Priam's aid, and rescue of his town.
Unhappy he! that would no credit give
Unto his spouse's words of prophecy.
    Whom when I saw, assembled in such wise,
So desperately the battle to desire;
Then furthermore thus said I unto them:
'O! ye young men, of courage stout in vain!
For nought ye strive to save the burning town.
What cruel fortune hath betid, ye see!
The Gods out of the temples all are fled,
Through whose might long this empire was main-
        tain'd:
Their altars eke are left both waste and void.
But if your will be bent with me to prove
That uttermost, that now may us befall;
Then let us die, and run amid our foes.
To vanquish'd folk, despair is only hope.'
    With this the young men's courage did increase;
And through the dark, like to the ravening wolves
Whom raging fury of their empty maws
Drives from their den, leaving with hungry throats

Their whelps behind; among our foes we ran,
Upon their swords, unto apparent death;
Holding alway the chief street of the town,
Cover'd with the close shadows of the night.
    Who can express the slaughter of that night?
Or tell the number of the corpses slain?
Or can in tears bewail them worthily?
The ancient famous city falleth down,
That many years did hold such seignory.
With senseless bodies every street is spread,
Each palace, and sacred porch of the gods.
Nor yet alone the Troyan blood was shed.
Manhood ofttimes into the vanquish'd breast
Returns, whereby some victors Greeks are slain.
Cruel complaints, and terror everywhere,
And plenty of grisly pictures of death.
    And first with us Androgeus there met,
Fellowed[1] with a swarming rout of Greeks,
Deeming us, unware, of that fellowship,
With friendly words whom thus he call'd unto:
' Haste ye, my friends! what sloth hath tarried you?
Your feres now sack and spoil the burning Troy:
From the tall ships where ye but newly come.'
    When he had said, and heard no answer made
To him again, whereto he might give trust;
Finding himself chanced amid his foes,
'Maz'd he withdrew his foot back with his word:
Like him, that wand'ring in the bushes thick,
Treads on the adder with his reckless foot,
Reared for wrath, swelling her speckled neck,
Dismay'd, gives back all suddenly for fear:

---

[1] Perhaps "followed."

Androgeus so fear'd of that sight stept back,
And we gan rush amid the thickest rout;
When, here and there we did them overthrow,
Stricken with dread, unskilful of the place.
Our first labour thus lucked well with us.
 Chorebus then, encouraged by his chance,
Rejoicing said : ' Hold forth the way of health,
My feres, that hap and manhood hath us taught.
Change we our shields ; the Greeks' arms do we on :
Craft, or manhood, with foes what recks it which?
The slain to us their armour they shall yield.'
And with that word Androgeus' crested helm
And the rich arms of his shield did he on ;
A Greekish sword he girded by his side :
Like gladly Dimas and Ripheus did :
The whole youth gan them clad in the new spoils.
Mingled with Greeks, for no good luck to us,
We went, and gave many onsets that night,
And many a Greek we sent to Pluto's court.
Other there fled and hasted to their ships,
And to their coasts of safeguard ran again.
And some there were for shameful cowardry,
Clamb up again unto the hugy horse,
And did them hide in his well knowen womb.
 Ay me ! bootless it is for any wight
To hope on aught against will of the gods.
Lo ! where Cassandra, Priam's daughter dear,
From Pallas' church was drawn with sparkled tress,
Lifting in vain her flaming eyen to heaven ;
Her eyen, for fast her tender wrists were bound.
Which sight Chorebus raging could not bear,
Reckless of death, but thrust amid the throng ;
And after we through thickest of the swords.

Here were we first y-batter'd with the darts
Of our own feres, from the high temples' top;
Whereby of us great slaughter did ensue,
Mistaken by our Greekish arms and crests.
Then flock'd the Greeks moved with wrath and ire,
Of the Virgin from them so rescued.
The fell Ajax; and either Atrides,
And the great band cleped the Dolopes.
As wrestling winds, out of dispersed whirl
Befight themselves, the west with southern blast,
And gladsome east proud of Aurora's horse;
The woods do whiz; and foamy Nereus
Raging in fury, with three forked mace
From bottom's depth doth welter up the seas;
So came the Greeks.   And such, as by deceit
We sparkled erst in shadow of the night,
And drave about our town, appeared first:
Our feigned shields and weapons then they found,
And, by sound, our discording voice they knew.
We went to wreck with number overlaid.
And by the hand of Peneleus first
Chorebus fell before the altar dead
Of armed Pallas; and Rhipheus eke,
The justest man among the Troians all,
And he that best observed equity.
But otherwise it pleased now the Gods.
There Hypanis, and Dymas, both were slain;
Through pierced with the weapons of their feres.
Nor thee, Panthus, when thou wast overthrown,
Pity, nor zeal of good devotion,
Nor habit yet of Phœbus hid from scath.
    Ye Troyan ashes! and last flames of mine!
I call in witness, that at your last fall

K

I fled no stroke of any Greekish sword.
And if the fates would I had fallen in fight,
That with my hand I did deserve it well.
   With this from thence I was recoiled back
. With Iphytus and Pelias alone :
Iphytus weak, and feeble all for age ;
Pelias lamed by Ulysses' hand.
To Priam's palace cry did call us then:
Here was the fight right hideous to behold ;
As though there had no battle been but there,
Or slaughter made elsewhere throughout the town.
A fight of rage and fury there we saw.
The Greeks toward the palace rushed fast,
And cover'd with engines the gates beset,
And reared up ladders against the walls ;
Under the windows scaling by their steps,
Fenced with shields in their left hands, whereon
They did receive the darts; while their right hands
Griped for hold th' embattle of the wall.
The Troyans on the other part rend down
The turrets high, and eke the palace roof;
With such weapons they shope them to defend,
Seeing all lost, now at the point of death.
The gilt spars, and the beams then threw they
      down ;
Of old fathers the proud and royal works.
And with drawn swords some did beset the gates,
Which they did watch, and keep in routs full thick.
Our sprites restor'd to rescue the king's house,
To help them, and to give the vanquish'd strength.
   A postern with a blind wicket there was,
A common trade to pass through Priam's house ;
On the back side whereof waste houses stood :

Which way eft-sithes,[1] while that our kingdom
     dured,
Th' infortunate Andromache alone
Resorted to the parents of her make;
With young Astyanax, his grandsire to see.
Here passed I up to the highest tower,
From whence the wretched Troyans did throw
     down
Darts, spent in waste.   Unto a turret then
We stept, the which stood in a place aloft,
The top whereof did reach well near the stars ;
Where we were wont all Troyè to behold,
The Greekish navy, and their tents also.
With instruments of iron gan we pick,
To seek where we might find the joining shrunk
From that high seat; which we razed, and threw
     down :
Which falling, gave forthwith a rushing sound,
And large in breadth on Greekish routs it light.
But soon another sort stept in their stead ;
No stone unthrown, nor yet no dart uncast.
  Before the gate stood Pyrrhus in the porch
Rejoicing in his darts, with glittering arms ;
Like to th' adder with venemous herbès fed,
Whom cold winter all bolne, hid under ground ;
And shining bright, when she her slough had slung,
Her slipper back doth roll, with forked tongue
And raised breast, lift up against the sun.
With that together came great Periphas ;
Automedon eke, that guided had some time
Achilles' horse, now Pyrrhus armour bare ;
And eke with him the warlike Scyrian youth

    [1] Oft-times.

Assail'd the house; and threw flame to the top.
And he an axe before the foremost raught,
Wherewith he gan the strong gates hew, and break;
From whence he beat the staples out of brass,
He brake the bars, and through the timber pierc'd
So large a hole, whereby they might discern
The house, the court, and secret chambers eke
Of Priamus, and ancient kings of Troy;
And armed foes in th' entry of the gate.
　　But the palace within confounded was,
With wailing, and with rueful shrieks and cries;
The hollow halls did howl of women's plaint:
The clamour strake up to the golden stars.
The fray'd[1] mothers, wand'ring through the wide
　　　　house,
Embracing pillars, did them hold and kiss.
Pyrrhus assaileth with his father's might;
Whom the closures ne keepers might hold out.
With often pushed ram the gate did shake;
The posts beat down, removed from their hooks:
By force they made the way, and th' entry brake.
And now the Greeks let in, the foremost slew:
And the large palace with soldiers gan to fill.
Not so fiercely doth overflow the fields
The foaming flood, that breaks out of his banks;
Whose rage of waters bears away what heaps
Stand in his way, the cotes, and eke the herds.
As in th' entry of slaughter furious
I saw Pyrrhus, and either Atrides.
　　There Hecuba I saw, with a hundred mo'
Of her sons' wives, and Priam at the altar,

------

[1] Frightened.

Sprinkling with blood his flame of sacrifice.
Fifty bed-chambers of his children's wives,
With loss of so great hope of his offspring,
The pillars eke proudly beset with gold,
And with the spoils of other nations,
Fell to the ground: and what so that with flame
Untouched was, the Greeks did all possess.

Percase[1] you would ask what was Priam's fate?
When of his taken town he saw the chance,
And the gates of his palace beaten down,
His foes amid his secret chambers eke:
Th' old man in vain did on his shoulders then,
Trembling for age, his cuirass long disused:
His bootless sword he girded him about;
And ran amid his foes, ready to die.

Amid the court, under the heaven, all bare,
A great altar there stood, by which there grew
An old laurel tree, bowing thereunto,
Which with his shadow did embrace the gods.
Here Hecuba, with her young daughters all
About the altar swarmed were in vain;
Like doves, that flock together in the storm,
The statues of the Gods embracing fast.
But when she saw Priam had taken there
His armour, like as though he had been young:
' What furious thought my wretched spouse,'
          quod she,
' Did move thee now such weapons for to wield?
Why hastest thou?   This time doth not require
Such succour, ne yet such defenders now:
No, though Hector my son were here again.

[1] By chance.

Come hither; this altar shall save us all: .
Or we shall die together.'   Thus she said.
Wherewith she drew him back to her, and set
The aged man down in the holy seat.
    But lo! Polites, one of Priam's sons,
Escaped from the slaughter of Pyrrhus,
Comes fleeing through the weapons of his foes,
Searching, all wounded, the long galleries
And the void courts; whom Pyrrhus all in rage
Followed fast to reach a mortal wound;
And now in hand, well near strikes with his spear.
Who fleeing forth till he came now in sight
Of his parents, before their face fell down
Yielding the ghost with flowing streams of blood.
Priamus then, although he were half dead,
Might not keep in his wrath, nor yet his words;
But crieth out: 'For this thy wicked work,
And boldness eke such thing to enterprise,
If in the heavens any justice be,
That of such things takes any care or keep,
According thanks the Gods may yield to thee;
And send thee eke thy just deserved hire,
That made me see the slaughter of my child,
And with his blood defile the father's face.
But he, by whom thou feign'st thyself begot,
Achilles, was to Priam not so stern.
For, lo! he tend'ring my most humble suit,
The right, and faith, my Hector's bloodless corpse
Render'd, for to be laid in sepulture;
And sent me to my kingdom home again.'
    Thus said the aged man, and therewithal,
Forceless he cast his weak unwieldy dart:
Which repuls'd from the brass where it gave dint,

Without sound, hung vainly in the shield's boss.
Quod Pyrrhus: ' Then thou shalt this thing re-
        port :
On message to Pelide my father go ;
Shew unto him my cruel deed , and how
Neoptolem is swerved out of kind.
Now shalt thou die,' quod he.   And with that word
At the altar him trembling 'gan he draw
Wallowing through the bloodshed of his son :
And his left hand all clasped in his hair,
With his right arm drew forth his shining sword,
Which in his side he thrust up to the hilts.
Of Priamus this was the fatal fine,
The woful end that was allotted him,
When he had seen his palace all on flame,
With ruin of his Troyan turrets eke.
That royal prince of Asia, which of late
Reign'd over so many peoples and realms,
Like a great stock now lieth on the shore ;
His head and shoulders parted been in twain :
A body now without renown and fame.
    Then first in me enter'd the grisly fear :
Dismay'd I was.   Wherewith came to my mind
The image eke of my dear father, when
I thus beheld the king of equal age,
Yield up the spirit with wounds so cruelly.
Then thought I of Creusa left alone ;
And of my house in danger of the spoil,
And the estate of young Iulus eke.
I looked back to seek what number then
I might discern about me of my feres :
But wearied they had left me all alone.
Some to the ground were lopen from above,

Some in the flame their irked bodies cast.

There was no mo' but I left of them all,
When that I saw in Vesta's temple sit,
Dame Helen, lurking in a secret place;
(Such light the flame did give as I went by,
While here and there I cast mine eyen about :)
For she in dread lest that the Troians should
Revenge on her the ruin of their walls;
And of the Greeks the cruel wreaks also;
The fury eke of her forsaken make,
The common bane of Troy, and eke of Greece!
Hateful she sat beside the altars hid.
Then boil'd my breast with flame, and burning
  wrath,
To revenge my town, unto such ruin brought;
With worthy pains on her to work my will.
Thought I : "Shall she pass to the land of Sparte
All safe, and see Mycene her native land,
And like a queen return with victory
Home to her spouse, her parents, and children,
Followed with a train of Troyan maids,
And served with a band of Phrygian slaves;
A Priam eke with iron murder'd thus,
And Troyè town consumed all with flame,
Whose shore hath been so oft for-bathed in blood ?
No! no! for though on women the revenge
Unseemly is; such conquest hath no fame:
To give an end unto such mischief yet
My just revenge shall merit worthy praise;
And quiet eke my mind, for to be wroke [1]
On her which was the causer of this flame,
And satisfy the cinder of my feres.'

   [1] Avenged.

With furious mind while I did argue thus,
My blessed mother then appear'd to me,
Whom erst so bright mine eyes had never seen,
And with pure light she glistred in the night,
Disclosing her in form a goddess like,
As she doth seem to such as dwell in heaven.
My right hand then she took, and held it fast,
And with her rosy lips thus did she say:
' Son! what fury hath thus provoked thee
To such untamed wrath? what ragest thou?
Or where is now become the care of us?
Wilt thou not first go see where thou hast left
Anchises, thy father fordone with age?
Doth Creusa live, and Ascanius thy son?
Whom now the Greekish bands have round beset:
And were they not defenced by my cure,
Flame had them raught,[1] and en'mies' sword ere
         this.
Not Helen's beauty hateful unto thee,
Nor blamed Paris yet, but the Gods' wrath
Reft you this wealth, and overthrew your town.
Behold! (and I shall now the cloud remove,
Which overcast thy mortal sight doth dim;
Whose moisture doth obscure all things about:
And fear not thou to do thy mother's will,
Nor her advice refuse thou to perform :)
Here, where thou see'st the turrets overthrown,
Stone beat from stone, smoke rising mixt with dust,
Neptunus there shakes with his mace the walls,
And eke the loose foundations of the same,
And overwhelms the whole town from his seat:
And cruel Juno with the foremost here

[1] Reached.

Doth keep the gate that Scea cleped[1] is,
Near woode[2] for wrath, whereas she stands, and calls
In harness bright the Greeks out of their ships:
And in the turrets high behold where stands
Bright shining Pallas, all in warlike weed,
And with her shield, where Gorgon's head appears:
And Jupiter, my father, distributes
Availing strength, and courage to the Greeks;
Yet overmore, against the Troyan power
He doth provoke the rest of all the Gods.
Flee then, my son, and give this travail end;
Ne shall I thee forsake, in safeguard till
I have thee brought unto thy father's gate.'
This did she say: and therewith gan she hide
Herself, in shadow of the close night.
　　Then dreadful figures gan appear to me,
And great Gods eke aggrieved with our town.
I saw Troyè fall down in burning gledes;
Neptunus town, clean razed from the soil.
Like as the elm forgrown in mountains high,
Round hewen with axe, that husbandmen
With thick assaults strive to tear up, doth threat;
And hack'd beneath trembling doth bend his top,
Till yold[3] with strokes, giving the latter crack,
Rent from the height, with ruin it doth fall.
　　With this I went, and guided by a God
I passed through my foes, and eke the flame:
Their weapons and the fire eke gave me place.
And when that I was come before the gates,
And ancient building of my father's house;
My father, whom I hoped to convey
To the next hills, and did him thereto 'treat,

---

[1] Called.　　　[2] Furious.　　　[3] Yielded.

Refused either to prolong his life,
Or bide exile after the fall of Troy.
'All ye,' quod he, 'in whom young blood is fresh,
Whose strength remains entire and in full power,
Take ye your flight.
For if the Gods my life would have prorogued,
They had reserved for me this wonning place.[1]
It was enough, alas! and eke too much,
To see the town of Troy thus razed once;
To have lived after the city taken.
When ye have said, this corpse laid out forsake;
My hand shall seek my death, and pity shall
Mine en'mies move, or else hope of my spoil.
As for my grave, I weigh the loss but light:
For I my years, disdainful to the Gods,
Have lingered forth, unable to all needs,
Since that the sire of Gods and king of men
Strake me with thunder, and with levening blast.'
Such things he gan rehearse, thus firmly bent:
But we besprent with tears, my tender son,
And eke my sweet Creusa, with the rest
Of the household, my father 'gan beseech,
Not so with him to perish all at once,
Nor so to yield unto the cruel fate:
Which he refused, and stack to his intent.

    Driven I was to harness then again,
Miserably my death for to desire.
For what advice, or other hope was left?
'Father! thought'st thou that I may once remove,'
Quod I, 'a foot, and leave thee here behind?
May such a wrong pass from a father's mouth?
If God's will be, that nothing here be saved

[1] Dwelling-place.

Of this great town, and thy mind bent to join
Both thee and thine to ruin of this town :
The way is plain this death for to attain.
Pyrrhus shall come besprent with Priam's blood,
That gor'd the son before the father's face,
And slew the father at the altar eke.
O sacred Mother ! was it then for this
That you me led through flame, and weapons sharp,
That I might in my secret chamber see
Mine en'mies ; and Ascanius my son,
My father, with Creusa my sweet wife,
Murder'd, alas ! the one in th' others' blood ?
Why, servants ! then, bring me my arms again.
The latter day us vanquished doth call.
Render me now to the Greeks' sight again :
And let me see the fight begun of new ;
We shall not all unwroken[1] die this day.'
  About me then I girt my sword again,
And eke my shield on my left shoulder cast,
And bent me so to rush out of the house.
Lo ! in my gate my spouse, clasping my feet,
For against his father young Iulus set.
' If thou wilt go,' quod she, ' and spill thyself,
Take us with thee in all that may betide.
But as expert if thou in arms have set
Yet any hope, then first this house defend,
Whereas thy son, and eke thy father dear,
And I, sometime thine own dear wife, are left.'
Her shrill loud voice with plaint thus fill'd the
          house ;
When that a sudden monstrous marvel fell :
For in their sight, and woful parents' arms,

[1] Unrevenged.

Behold a light out of the button sprang
That in tip of Iulus cap did stand;
With gentle touch whose harmless flame did shine
Upon his hair, about his temples spread.
And we afraid, trembling for dreadful fear,
Bet out the fire from his blazing tress,
And with water 'gan quench the sacred flame.
    Anchises glad his eyen lift to the stars;
With hands his voice to heaven thus he bent.
' If by prayer, almighty Jupiter,
Inclined thou mayst be, behold us then
Of ruth[1] at least, if we so much deserve.
Grant eke thine aid, Father! confirm this thing.
    Scarce had the old man said, when that the
        heavens
With sudden noise thunder'd on the left hand:
Out of the sky, by the dark night there fell
A blazing star, dragging a brand or flame,
Which with much light gliding on the house top,
In the forest of Ida hid her beams;
The which full bright cendleing[2] a furrow, shone,
By a long tract appointing us the way;
And round about of brimstone rose a fume.
    My father vanquish'd then, beheld the skies,
Spake to the Gods, and th' holy star adored:
' Now, now,' quod he, ' no longer I abide:
Follow I shall where ye my guide at hand.
O native Gods! your family defend;
Preserve your line, this warning comes of you,
And Troyè stands in your protection now.
Now give I place, and whereso that thou go,
Refuse I not, my son, to be thy fere.'

[1] Of pity.   [2] Kindling.

This did he say; and by that time more clear
The cracking flame was heard throughout the walls,
And more and more the burning heat drew near.
'Why then! have done, my father dear,' quod I,
'Bestride my neck forthwith, and sit thereon,
And I shall with my shoulders thee sustain,
Ne shall this labour do me any dere.
What so betide, come peril, come welfare,
Like to us both and common there shall be.
Young Iulus shall bear me company;
And my wife shall follow far off my steps.
Now ye, my servants, mark well what I say:
Without the town ye shall find, on a hill,
An old temple there stands, whereas some time
Worship was done to Ceres the Goddess;
Beside which grows an aged cypress tree,
Preserved long by our forefathers' zeal:
Behind which place let us together meet.
And thou, Father, receive into thy hands
The reliques all, and the Gods of the land:
The which it were not lawful I should touch,
That come but late from slaughter and bloodshed,
Till I be washed in the running flood.'
When I had said these words, my shoulders broad,
And laied neck with garments 'gan I spread,
And thereon cast a yellow lion's skin;
And thereupon my burden I receive.
Young Iulus clasped in my right hand,
Followeth me fast with unegal pace;
And at my back my wife.   Thus did we pass
By places shadowed most with the night.
And me, whom late the dart which enemies threw,
Nor press of Argive routs could make amaz'd,

Each whisp'ring wind hath power now to fray,
And every sound to move my doubtful mind:
So much I dread my burden, and my fere.

And now we 'gan draw near unto the gate,
Right well escap'd the danger, as me thought,
When that at hand a sound of feet we heard.
My father then, gazing throughout the dark,
Cried on me, ' Flee, son ! they are at hand.'
With that bright shields, and shene armours I saw.
But then I know not what unfriendly God
My troubled wit from me bereft for fear :
For while I ran by the most secret streets,
Eschewing still the common haunted track,
From me catif, alas ! bereaved was
Creusa then, my spouse, I wot not how ;
Whether by fate, or missing of the way,
Or that she was by weariness retain'd :
But never sith these eyes might her behold ;
Nor did I yet perceive that she was lost,
Ne never backward turned I my mind,
Till we came to the hill, whereas there stood
The old temple dedicate to Ceres.

And when that we were there assembled all,
She was only away, deceiving us
Her spouse, her son, and all her company.
What God or man did I not then accuse,
Near woode for ire ? or what more cruel chance
Did hap to me, in all Troy's overthrow ?
Ascanius to my feres I then betook,
With Anchises, and eke the Troyan Gods.
And left them hid within a valley deep.
And to the town I 'gan me hie again,
Clad in bright arms, and bent for to renew

Aventures past, to search throughout the town,
And yield my head to perils once again.
  And first the walls and dark entry I sought
Of the same gate whereat I issued out;
Holding backward the steps where we had come
In the dark night, looking all round about:
In every place the ugsome sights I saw;
The silence self of night, aghast my sprite.
From hence again I pass'd unto our house,
If she by chance had been returned home.
The Greeks were there, and had it all beset:
The wasting fire, blown up by drift of wind,
Above the roofs the blazing flame sprang up;
The sound whereof with fury pierced the skies.
To Priam's palace, and the castle then
I made; and there at Juno's sanctuair,
In the void porches, Phenix, Ulysses eke
Stern guardians stood, watching of the spoil.
The riches here were set, reft from the brent
Temples of Troy: the tables of the Gods,
The vessels eke that were of massy gold,
And vestures spoil'd, were gather'd all in heap:
The children orderly, and mothers pale for fright,
Long ranged on a row stood round about.
  So bold was I to show my voice that night
With clepes and cries to fill the streets through-
     out,
With Creuse' name in sorrow, with vain tears;
And often sithes the same for to repeat.
The town restless with fury as I sought,
Th' unlucky figure of Creusa's ghost,
Of stature more than wont, stood 'fore mine eyen.
Abashed then I woxe: therewith my hair

'Gan start right up : my voice stack in my throat :
When with such words she 'gan my heart remove :
' What helps, to yield unto such furious rage,
Sweet spouse ?' quod she, ' Without will of the
      Gods
This chanced not : ne lawful was for thee
To lead away Creusa hence with thee :
The King of the high heaven suff'reth it not.
A long exile thou art assigned to bear,
Long to furrow large space of stormy seas :
So shalt thou reach at last Hesperian land,
Where Lidian Tiber with his gentle stream
Mildly doth flow along the fruitful fields.
There mirthful wealth, there kingdom is for thee ;
There a king's child prepar'd to be thy make.
For thy beloved Creusa stint thy tears :
For now shall I not see the proud abodes
Of Myrmidons, nor yet of Dolopes :
Ne I, a Troyan lady, and the wife
Unto the son of Venus, the Goddess,
Shall go a slave to serve the Greekish dames.
Me here the God's great mother holds.——
And now farewell : and keep in father's breast
The tender love of thy young son and mine.'
    This having said, she left me all in tears,
And minding much to speak ; but she was gone,
And subtly fled into the weightless air.
Thrice raught I with mine arms t' accoll[1] her neck :
Thrice did my hands vain hold th' image escape,
Like nimble winds, and like the flying dream.
So night spent out, return I to my feres ;
And there wond'ring I find together swarm'd

[1] To embrace.

L

A new number of mates, mothers, and men,
A rout exiled, a wretched multitude,
From each-where flock together, prest to pass
With heart and goods, to whatsoever land
By sliding seas, me listed them to lead.
And now rose Lucifer above the ridge
Of lusty Ide, and brought the dawning light.
The Greeks held th' entries of the gates beset:
Of help there was no hope.   Then gave I place,
Took up my sire, and hasted to the hill.

THE FOURTH BOOK OF VIRGIL'S
ÆNEID.

UT now the wounded Queen, with
heavy care,
Throughout the veins she nourisheth
the plaie,
Surprised with blind flame; and to
her mind
'Gan eke resort the prowess of the man,
And honour of his race: while in her breast
Imprinted stack his words, and pictures form.
Ne to her limbs care granteth quiet rest.
The next morrow, with Phœbus' lamp the earth
Alighted clear; and eke the dawning day
The shadows dark 'gan from the pole remove:
When all unsound, her sister of like mind
Thus spake she to: 'O! Sister Anne, what dreams
Be these, that me tormented thus affray?
What new guest is this, that to our realm is come?
What one of cheer? how stout of heart in arms?
Truly I think (ne vain is my belief)
Of Goddish race some offspring should he be:

Cowardry notes hearts swerved out of kind.
He driven, lord! with how hard destiny!
What battles eke achieved did he recount!
But that my mind is fixt unmovably,
Never with wight in wedlock aye to join,
Sith my first love me left by death dissever'd ;
If genial brands and bed me loathed not,
To this one guilt perchance yet might I yield.
Anne, for I grant, sith wretched Sichee's death,
My spouse and house with brother's slaughter
        stain'd,
This only man hath made my senses bend,
And pricked forth the mind that 'gan to slide :
Now feelingly I taste the steps of mine old flame.
But first I wish the earth me swallow down,
Or with thunder the mighty Lord me send
To the pale ghosts of hell, and darkness deep ;
Ere I thee stain, shamefastness, or thy laws.
He that with me first coupled, took away
My love with him ; enjoy it in his grave.'
    Thus did she say, and with supprised tears
Bained her breast. Whereto Anne thus replied :
' O Sister, dearer beloved than the light :
Thy youth alone in plaint still wilt thou spill ?
Ne children sweet, ne Venus' gifts wilt know ?
Cinders, thinkest thou, mind this ? or graved ghosts ?
Time of thy doole,[1] thy spouse new dead, I grant,
None might thee move : no, not the Libyan king,
Nor yet of Tyre ; Iarbas set so light,
And other princes mo' ; whom the rich soil
Of Afric breeds, in honours triumphant.
Wilt thou also gainstand thy liked love ?

            [1] Dole, or grief.

Comes not to mind upon whose land thou dwell'st ?
On this side, lo ! the Getule town behold,
A people bold, unvanquished in war;
Eke the undaunted Numides compass thee ;
Also the Sirtes unfriendly harbrough.
On th' other hand, a desert realm for-thrust,
The Barceans, whose fury stretcheth wide.
What shall I touch the wars that move from Tyre ?
Or yet thy brother's threats ?——
By Gods purveyance it blew, and Juno's help,
The Troiaynes ships, I think, to run this course.
Sister, what town shalt thou see this become ?
Through such ally how shall our kingdom rise ?
And by the aid of Troyan arms how great ?
How many ways shall Carthages glory grow ?
Thou only now beseech the Gods of grace
By sacrifice : which ended, to thy house
Receive him, and forge causes of abode :
Whiles winter frets the seas, and wat'ry Orion,
The ships shaken, unfriendly the season.'
    Such words inflamed the kindled mind with love,
Loosed all shame, and gave the doubtful hope.
And to the temples first they haste, and seek
By sacrifice for grace, with hogrels[1] of two years,
Chosen, as ought, to Ceres that gave laws,
To Phœbus, Bacchus, and to Juno chief,
Which hath in care the bands of marriage.
Fair Dido held in her right hand the cup,
Which 'twixt the horns of a white cow she shed
In presence of the Gods, passing before
The altars fat ; which she renewed oft
With gifts that day, and beasts deboweled ;

                    [2] Sheep two years old. .

Gazing for counsel on the entrails warm.
Ay me! unskilful minds of prophesy!
Temples or vows, what boot they in her rage?
A gentle flame the marrow doth devour,
Whiles in the breast the silent wound keeps life.
Unhappy Dido burns, and in her rage
Throughout the town she wand'reth up and down.
Like the stricken hind with shaft, in Crete
Throughout the woods which chasing with his dart
Aloof, the shepherd smiteth at unwares,
And leaves unwist in her the thirling head:
That through the groves, and lands glides in her
        flight;
Amid whose side the mortal arrow sticks.
    Æneas now about the walls she leads,
The town prepared, and Carthage wealth to shew,
Off'ring to speak, amid her voice, she whists.
And when the day gan fail new feasts she makes;
The Troies travails to hear a-new she lists,
Enraged all; and stareth in his face
That tells the tale. And when they were all gone,
And the dim moon doth eft withhold the light,
And sliding stars provoked unto sleep;
Alone she mourns within her palace void,
And sets her down on her forsaken bed.
And, absent, him she bears, when he is gone,
And seeth eke.   Oft in her lap she holds
Ascanius, trapp'd by his father's form:
So to beguile the love, cannot be told.
    The turrets now arise not, erst begun;
Neither the youth wields arms, nor they advance
The ports, nor other meet defence for war:
Broken there hang the works and mighty frames

Of walls high raised, threatening the sky.
Whom as soon as Jove's dear wife saw infect
With such a plague, ne fame resist the rage;
Saturnès' daughter thus burdes Venus then:
'Great praise,' quod she, 'and worthy spoils you
      win,
You and your son; great Gods of memory!
By both your wiles one woman to devour.
Yet am not I deceived, that foreknew
Ye dread our walls, and buildings gan suspect
Of high Carthage.   But what shall be the end?
Or whereunto now serveth such debate?
But rather peace, and bridal bands knit we,
Sith thou hast sped of that thy heart desired;
Dido doth burn with love: rage frets her bones,
This people now as common to us both,
With equal favour let us govern then;
Lawful be it to serve a Trojan spouse;
And Tyrians yield to thy right hand in dower.'
   To whom Venus replied thus, that knew
Her words proceeded from a feigned mind,
To Libyan coasts to turn th' empire from Rome.
'What wight so fond such offer to refuse?
Or yet with thee had liever[1] strive in war?
So be it fortune thy tale bring t' effect:
But destinies I doubt; lest Jove nill[2] grant,
That folk of Tyre, and such as came from Troy,
Should hold one town; or grant these nations
Mingled to be, or joined aye in league.
Thou art his wife: lawful it is for thee
For to attempt his fancy by request:
Pass on before; and follow thee I shall.'

    [1] Rather.   [2] Will not.

Queen Juno then thus took her tale again:
' This travail be it mine.   But by what mean
(Mark, in few words I shall thee learn eftsoons,)
This work in hand may now be compassed.
Æneas now, and wretched Dido eke,
To the forest a hunting mind to wend
To-morn, as soon as Titan shall ascend,
And with his beams hath overspread the world:
And whiles the wings of youth do swarm about,
And whiles they range to overset the groves,
A cloudy shower mingled with hail I shall
Pour down, and then with thunder shake the skies.
Th' assembly scattered the mist shall cloke.
Dido a cave, the Troyan prince the same
Shall enter too; and I will be at hand:
And if thy will stick unto mine, I shall
In wedlock sure knit, and make her his own:
Thus shall the marriage be.'   To whose request
Without debate Venus did seem to yield,
And smiled soft, as she that found the wile.

   Then from the seas the dawning gan arise:
The sun once up, the chosen youth gan throng
Out at the gates: the hayes so rarely knit,
The hunting staves with their broad heads of steel;
And of Masile the horsemen forth they brake;
Of scenting hounds a kennel huge likewise.
And at the threshold of her chamber door
The Carthage lords did on the Queen attend.
The trampling steed, with gold and purple trapp'd,
Chawing the foamy bit, there fiercely stood.
Then issued she, awaited with great train,
Clad in a cloak of Tyre embroider'd rich.
Her quiver hung behind her back, her tress

Knotted in gold, her purple vesture eke
Button'd with gold.   The Troyans of her train
Before her go, with gladsome Iulus.
Æneas eke, the goodliest of the rout,
Makes one of them, and joineth close the throngs:
Like when Apollo leaveth Lycia,
His wint'ring place, and Xanthus' floods likewise,
To visit Delos, his mother's mansion,
Repairing eft and furnishing her choir:
The Candians, and folks of Driopes,
With painted Agathyrsies shout, and cry,
Environing the altars round about;
When that he walks upon mount Cynthus' top:
His sparkled tress repress'd with garlands soft
Of tender leaves, and trussed up in gold;
His quivering darts clatt'ring behind his back.
So fresh and lusty did Æneas seem;
Such lordly port in present countenance.
   But to the hills and wild holts when they came;
From the rock's top the driven savage rose.
Lo from the hill above, on th' other side,
Through the wide lawns they gan to take their
          course.
The harts likewise in troops taking their flight,
Raising the dust, the mountain-fast forsake.
The child Iulus, blithe of his swift steed,
Amid the plain now pricks by them, now these;
And to encounter wisheth oft in mind
The foaming Boar, instead of fearful beasts,
Or Lion brown, might from the hill descend.
   In the mean while the skies gan rumble sore;
In tail thereof, a mingled shower with hail.
The Tyrian folk, and eke the Troyans youth.

And Venus' nephew the cottages, for fear,
Sought round about; the floods fell from the hills.
Dido a den, the Troyan prince the same,
Chanced upon.   Our mother then, the Earth,
And Juno that hath charge of marriage,
First tokens gave with burning gleads of flame;
And, privy to the wedlock, lightning skies;
And the Nymphs yelled from the mountains top.
   Ay me! this was the first day of their mirth,
And of their harms the first occasion eke.
Respect of fame no longer her withholds:
Nor museth now to frame her love by stealth.
Wedlock she calls it: under the pretence
Of which fair name she cloaketh now her fault.
   Forthwith Flame flieth through the great Libyan
        towns:
A mischief Fame, there is none else so swift;
That moving grows, and flitting gathers force.
First small for dread, soon after climbs the skies;
Stayeth on earth, and hides her head in clouds.
Whom our mother the earth, tempted by wrath
Of Gods, begat; the last Sister (they write)
To Cäeus, and to Enceladus eke:
Speedy of foot, of wing likewise as swift,
A monster huge, and dreadful to descrive.[1]
In every plume that on her body sticks
(A thing indeed much marvelous to hear)
As many waker eyes lurk underneath,
So many mouths to speak, and listening ears.
By night she flies amid the cloudy sky,
Shrieking, by the dark shadow of the earth,
Ne doth decline to the sweet sleep her eyes.

[1] Describe.

By day she sits to mark on the house top,
Or turrets high; and the great towns affrays;
As mindful of ill and lies, as blasing truth.
   This monster blithe with many a tale gan sow
This rumour then into the common ears:
As well things done, as that was never wrought:
As, that there comen is to Tyrian's court
Æneas, one outsprung of Troyan blood,
To whom fair Dido would herself be wed:
And that, the while, the winter long they pass
In foul delight, forgetting charge of reign;
Led against honour with unhonest lust.
   This in each mouth the filthy Goddess spreads;
And takes her course to king Hiarbas straight,
Kindling his mind; with tales she feeds his wrath;
Gotten was he by Ammon Jupiter
Upon the ravish'd nymph of Garamant.
A hundred hugy, great temples he built
In his far stretching realms to Jupiter;
Altars as many kept with waking flame,
A watch always upon the Gods to tend;
The floors embru'd with yielded blood of beasts,
And threshold spread with garlands of strange hue.
He woode[1] of mind, kindled by bitter bruit
Tofore[2] th' altars, in presence of the Gods,
With reared hands gan humbly Jove entreat:
  'Almighty God! whom the Moores nation
Fed at rich tables presenteth with wine,
See'st thou these things? or fear we thee in vain,
When thou lettest fly thy thunder from the clouds?
Or do those flames with vain noise us affray?
A woman, that wandering in our coasts hath bought

---

[1] Mad, furious.   [2] Before.

A plot for price, where she a city set;
To whom we gave the strond for to manure,
And laws to rule her town, our wedlock loathed,
Hath chose Æneas to command her realm.
That Paris now, with his unmanly sort,
With mitred hats, with ointed bush and beard,
His rape enjoyeth: whiles to thy temples we
Our offerings bring, and follow rumours vain.'
   Whom praying in such sort, and griping eke
The altars fast, the mighty father heard;
And writhed his look toward the royal walls,
And lovers eke, forgetting their good name.
To Mercury then gave he thus in charge:
' Hence, son, in haste! and call to thee the winds;
Slide with thy plumes, and tell the Troyan prince
That now in Carthage loitereth, rechless
Of the towns granted him by destiny.
Swift through the skies see thou these words convey:
His fair Mother behight him not to us
Such one to be; ne therefore twice him saved
From Greekish arms: but such a one
As meet might seem great Italy to rule,
Dreadful in arms, charged with seigniory,
Shewing in proof his worthy Teucrian race;
And under laws the whole world to subdue.
If glory of such things nought him enflame,
Ne that he lists seek honour by some pain;
The towers yet of Rome, being his sire,
Doth he envy to young Ascanius?
What mindeth he to frame? or on what hope
In en'mies land doth he make his abode?
Ne his offspring in Italy regards?
Ne yet the land of Lavine doth behold?

Bid him make sail: have here the sum and end;
Our message thus report.'   When Jove had said,
Then Mercury 'gan bend him to obey
His mighty father's will: and to his heels
His golden wings he knits, which him transport,
With a light wind above the earth and seas.
And then with him his wand he took, whereby
He calls from hell pale ghosts; and other some
Thither also he sendeth comfortless:
Whereby he forceth sleeps, and them bereaves;
And mortal eyes he closeth up in death.
By power whereof he drives the winds away,
And passeth eke amid the troubled clouds,
Till in his flight he gan descry the top
And the steep flanks of rocky Atlas' hill,
That with his crown sustains the welkin up:
Whose head forgrown with pine, circled alway
With misty clouds, is beaten with wind and storm;
His shoulders spread with snow; and from his chin
The springs descend; his beard frozen with ice.
Here Mercury with equal shining wings
First touched; and with body headling bet,
To the water then took he his descent:
Like to the fowl that endlong coasts and stronds
Swarming with fish, flies sweeping by the sea;
Cutting betwixt the winds and Libyan lands,
From his grandfather by the mother's side,
Cyllène's child so came, and then alight
Upon the houses with his winged feet;
Tofore the towers where he Æneas saw
Foundations cast, arearing lodges new;
Girt with a sword of jasper, starry bright;
A shining 'parel, flamed with stately eye

Of Tyrian purple, hung his shoulders down,
The gift and work of wealthy Dido's hand,
Striped throughout with a thin thread of gold.
   Thus he encounters him: ' Oh careless wight !
Both of thy realm, and of thine own affairs ;
A wife-bound man now dost thou rear the walls
Of high Carthage, to build a goodly town !
From the bright skies the ruler of the Gods
Sent me to thee, that with his beck commands
Both heav'n and earth : in haste he gave me charge
Through the light air this message thee to say.
What framest thou ? or on what hope thy time
In idleness dost waste in Afric land ?
Of so great things if nought the fame thee stir,
Ne list by travail honour to pursue ;
Ascanius yet, that waxeth fast, behold ;
And the hope of Iulus' seed, thine heir ;
To whom the realm of Italy belongs,
And soil of Rome.' When Mercury had said,
Amid his tale far off from mortal eyes
Into light air he vanish'd out of sight.
   Æneas with that vision striken down,
Well near bestraught,[1] upstart his hair for dread,
Amid his throatal his voice likewise 'gan stick.
For to depart by night he longeth now,
And the sweet land to leave, astoined sore
With this advise and message of the Gods.
What may he do, alas ! or by what words
Dare he persuade the raging Queen in love ?
Or in what sort may he his tale begin ?
Now here, now there his rechless mind 'gan run,
And diversely him draws, discoursing all.

     [1] Distracted.

After long doubts this sentence seemed best:
Mnestheus first, and strong Cloanthus eke
He calls to him, with Sergest; unto whom
He gave in charge his navy secretly
For to prepare, and drive to the sea coast
His people; and their armour to address;
And for the cause of change to feign excuse:
And that he, when good Dido least foreknew,
Or did suspect so great a love could break,
Would wait his time to speak thereof most meet;
The nearest way to hasten his intent.
Gladly his will and biddings they obey.

 Full soon the Queen this crafty sleight 'gan smell,
(Who can deceive a lover in forecast?)
And first foresaw the motions for to come;
Things most assured fearing.   Unto whom
That wicked Fame reported, how to flight
Was arm'd the fleet, all ready to avale.
Then ill bested of counsel, rageth she;
And whisketh through the town: like Bacchus' nun,
As Thyas stirs, the sacred rites begun,
And when the wonted third years sacrifice
Doth prick her forth, hearing Bacchus' name hal-
 lowed,
And that the feastful night of Citheron
Doth call her forth, with noise of dancing.

 At length herself bordeth Æneas thus:
'Unfaithful wight! to cover such a fault
Couldest thou hope? unwist to leave my land?
Not thee our love, nor yet right hand betrothed,
Ne cruel death of Dido may withhold?
But that thou wilt in winter ships prepare,
And try the seas in broil of whirling winds?

What if the land thou seekest were not strange!
If not unknowen? or ancient Troy yet stood?
In rough seas yet should Troye town be sought?
Shunnest thou me? By these tears, and right hand,
(For nought else have I, wretched, left myself)
By our spousals and marriage begun,
If I of thee deserved ever well,
Or thing of mine were ever to thee lief;
Rue on this realm, whose ruin is at hand.
If ought be left that prayer may avail,
I thee beseech to do away this mind.
The Libyans, and tyrants of Nomadane,
For thee me hate: my Tyrians eke for thee
Are wroth; by thee my shamefastness eke stained,
And good renown, whereby up to the stars
Peerless I clamb.   To whom wilt thou me leave,
Ready to die, my sweet guest? sith this name
Is all, as now, that of a spouse remains.
But whereto now should I prolong my death?
What! until my brother Pigmalion
Beat down my walls? or the Getulian king
Hiarbas, yet captive lead me away?
Before thy flight a child had I once borne,
Or seen a young Æneas in my court
Play up and down, that might present thy face,
All utterly I could not seem forsaken.'
    Thus said the Queen.   He to the God's advice,
Unmoved held his eyes, and in his breast
Represt his care, and strove against his will:
And these few words at last then forth he cast.
' Never shall I deny, Queen, thy desert;
Greater than thou in words may well express.
To think on thee ne irk me aye it shall,

Whiles of myself I shall have memory ;
And whiles the spirit these limbs of mine shall rule.
For present purpose somewhat shall I say.
Never meant I to cloak the same by stealth,
Slander me not, ne to escape by flight :
Nor I to thee pretended marriage;
Ne hither came to join me in such league.
If destiny at mine own liberty,
To lead my life would have permitted me,
After my will, my sorrow to redoub,[1]
Troy and the remainder of our folk
Restore I should : and with these scaped hands,
The walls again unto these vanquished,
And palace high of Priam eke repair.
But now Apollo, called Grineus,
And prophecies of Lycia me advise
To seize upon the realm of Italy :
That is my love, my country, and my land.
If Carthage turrets thee, Phœnician born,
And of a Libyan town the sight detain ;   .
To us Troyans why doest thou then envy
In Italy to make our resting seat ?
Lawful is eke for us strange realms to seek.
As oft as night doth cloak with shadows dark
The earth, as oft as flaming stars appear,
The troubled ghost of my father Anchises
So oft in sleep doth fray me, and advise :
The wronged head by me of my dear son,
Whom I defraud of the Hesperian crown,
And lands allotted him by destiny.
The messenger eke of the Gods but late
Sent down from Jove (I swear by either head)

[1] Redub, to remedy, redress.

M

Passing the air, did this to me report.
In bright day-light the God myself I saw
Enter these walls, and with these ears him heard.
Leave then with plaint to vex both thee and me:
Against my will to Italy I go.'
    Whiles in this sort he did his tale pronounce,
With wayward look she 'gan him aye behold,
And rolling eyes, that moved to and fro ;
With silent look discoursing over all :
And forth in rage at last thus 'gan she upbraid :
    'Faithless ! forsworn ! ne Goddess was thy dam !
Nor Dardanus beginner of thy race !
But of hard rocks mount Caucase monstruous
Bred thee, and teats of tyger gave thee suck.
But what should I dissemble now my cheer ?
Or me reserve to hope of greater things ?
Minds he our tears ? or ever moved his eyen ?
Wept he for ruth ? or pitied he our love ?
What shall I set before ? or where begin ?
Juno, nor Jove with just eyes this beholds.
Faith is no where in surety to be found.
Did I not him, thrown up upon my shore
In need receive, and fonded eke invest
Of half my realm ? his navy lost, repair ?
From death's danger his fellows eke defend ?
Ay me ! with rage and furies, lo ! I drive.
Apollo now, now Lycian prophecies,
Another while, the messenger of Gods,
He says, sent down from mighty Jove himself.
The dreadful charge amid the skies hath brought.
As though that were the travail of the Gods,
Or such a care their quietness might move !
I hold thee not, nor yet gainsay thy words :

To Italy pass on by help of winds;
And through the floods go search thy kingdom new.
If ruthful Gods have any power, I trust
Amid the rocks thy guerdon thou shalt find;
When thou shalt clepe full oft on Dido's name.
With burial brandes I, absent, shall thee chase:
And when cold death from life these limbs divides,
My ghost each where shall still on thee await.
Thou shalt abye[1]; and I shall hear thereof,
Among the souls below the bruit shall come.'
  With such like words she cut off half her tale,
With pensive heart abandoning the light.
And from his sight herself gan far remove;
Forsaking him, that many things in fear
Imagined, and did prepare to say.
Her swouning limbs her damsels 'gan relieve,
And to her chamber bare of marble stone;
And laid her on her bed with tapets[2] spread.
  But just Æneas, though he did desire
With comfort sweet her sorrows to appease,
And with his words to banish all her care;
Wailing her much, with great love overcome:
The Gods' will yet he worketh, and resorts
Unto his navy.   Where the Troyans fast
Fell to their work, from the shore to unstock
High rigged ships: now fletes the tallowed keel;
Their oars with leaves yet green from wood they
       bring;
And masts unshave for haste, to take their flight.
You might have seen them throng out of the town
Like ants, when they do spoil the bing of corn,

[1] To expiate, to pay for.
[2] Cloth of any kind, as tapestry.

For winter's dread, which they bear to their den :
When the black swarm creeps over all the fields,
And thwart the grass by strait paths drags their prey ·
The great grains then some on their shoulders truss,
Some drive the troop, some chastise eke the slow :
That with their travail chafed is each path.

Beholding this, what thought might Dido have ?
What sighs gave she ? when from her towers high
The large coasts she saw haunted with Troyan's
        works,
And in her sight the seas with din confounded ?
O, witless Love ! what thing is that to do
A mortal mind thou canst not force thereto ?
Forced she is to tears ay to return,
With new requests to yield her heart to love :
And lest she should before her causeless death
Leave any thing untried : 'O sister Anne !'
Quoth she, ' behold the whole coast round about,
How they prepare, assembled every where ;
The streaming sails abiding but for wind :
The shipmen crown their ships with boughs for joy.
O sister ! if so great a sorrow I
Mistrusted had, it were more light to bear.
Yet natheless this for me wretched wight,
Anne, shalt thou do : for faithless, thee alone
He reverenced, thee eke his secrets told ;
The meetest time thou knowest to borde the man :
To my proud foe thus, sister, humbly say ;
I with the Greeks within the port Aulide
Conjured not, the Troyans to destroy ;
Nor to the walls of Troy yet sent my fleet :
Nor cinders of his father Anchises
Disturbed have, out of his sepulture.

Why lets he not my words sink in his ears
So hard to overtreat ?   Whither whirls he ?
This last boon yet grant he to wretched love.
Prosperous winds for to depart with ease
Let him abide ; the foresaid marriage now,
That he betray'd, I do not him require ;
Nor that he should fair Italy forgo :
Neither I would he should his kingdom leave.
Quiet I ask, and a time of delay,
And respite eke my fury to assuage,
Till my mishap teach me, all comfortless,
How for to wail my grief.   This latter grace,
Sister, I crave : have thou remorse of me ;
Which, if thou shalt vouchsafe, with heaps I shall
Leave by my death redoubled unto thee.'
   Moisted with tears thus wretched 'gan she plain :
Which Anne reports, and answer brings again.
Nought tears him move, ne yet to any words
He can be framed with gentle mind to yield.
The Werdes[1] withstand, a God stops his meek ears.
Like to the aged boisteous bodied oak,
The which among the Alps the Northern winds
Blowing now from this quarter, now from that,
Betwixt them strive to overwhelm with blasts :
The whistling air among the branches roars,
Which all at once bow to the earth her crops,
The stock once smit : whiles in the rocks the tree
Sticks fast ; and look, how high to the heav'n her top
Rears up, so deep her root spreads down to hell.
So was this Lord now here now there beset
With words ; in whose stout breast wrought many
      cares.

[1] The Fates.

But still his mind in one remains; in vain
The tears were shed.   Then Dido, fray'd of Fates,
Wisheth for death, irked[1] to see the skies.
And that she might the rather work her will,
And leave the light, (a grisly thing to tell)
Upon the altars burning full of 'cense
When she set gifts of sacrifice, she saw
The holy water stocks wax black within;
The wine eke shed, change into filthy gore:
This she to none, not to her sister told.
A marble temple in her palace eke,
In memory of her old spouse, there stood,
In great honour and worship, which she held,
With snow white clothes deck'd, and with boughs
        of feast:
Whereout was heard her husband's voice, and speech
Cleping for her, when dark night hid the earth:
And oft the owl with rueful song complain'd
From the housetop, drawing long doleful tunes.
And many things forespoke by prophets past
With dreadful warning 'gan her now affray:
And stern Æneas seemed in her sleep
To chase her still about, distraught in rage:
And still her thought, that she was left alone
Uncompanied, great voyages to wend,
In desert land, her Tyrian folk to seek.
Like Pentheus, that in his madness saw
Swarming in flocks the furies all of hell;
Two suns remove, and Thebès town shew twain.
Or like Orestes Agamemnon's son, ·
In tragedies who represented aye
Is driven about, that from his mother fled

        [1] Wearied.

Armed with brands, and eke with serpent's black ;
That sitting found within the temple's porch
The ugly furies his slaughter to revenge.
   Yelden to woe, when phrensy had her caught,
Within herself then 'gan she well debate,
Full bent to die, the time and eke the mean ;
And to her woful sister thus she said,
In outward cheer dissembling her intent,
Presenting hope under a semblant glad :
   ' Sister, rejoice ! for I have found the way
Him to return, or loose me from his love.
Toward the end of the great ocean flood,
Whereas the wandering sun descendeth hence,
In the extremes of Ethiope, is a place
Where huge Atlas doth on his shoulders turn
The sphere so round with flaming stars beset.
Born of Massyle, I hear should be a Nun ;
That of the Hesperian sisters' temple old,
And of their goodly garden keeper was ;
That gives unto the Dragon eke his food,
That on the tree preserves the holy fruit ;
That honey moist, and sleeping poppy casts.
This woman doth avaunt, by force of charm,
What heart she list to set at liberty ;
And other some to pierce with heavy cares :
In running flood to stop the waters' course ;
And eke the stars their movings to reverse ;
T' assemble eke the ghosts that walk by night :
Under thy feet the earth thou shalt behold
Tremble and roar ; the oaks come from the hill.
The Gods and thee, dear sister, now I call
In witness, and thy head to me so sweet,
To magic arts against my will I bend.

Right secretly within our inner court,
In open air rear up a stack of wood ;
And hang thereon the weapon of this man,
The which he left within my chamber, stick :
His weeds dispoiled all, and bridal bed,
Wherein, alas ! Sister, I found my bane,
Charge thereupon ; for so the Nun commands,
To do away what did to him belong,
Of that false wight that might remembrance bring.'
   Then whisted she ; the pale her face 'gan stain.
Ne could yet Anne believe, her sister meant
To cloke her death by this new sacrifice ;
Nor in her breast such fury did conceive :
Neither doth she now dread more grievous thing
Than followed Sichées death ; wherefore
She put her will in ure.   But then the Queen,
When that the stack of wood was reared up
Under the air within the inward court
With cloven oak, and billets made of fir,
With garlands she doth all beset the place,
And with green boughs eke crown the funeral,
And thereupon his weeds and sword yleft,
And on a bed his picture she bestows,
As she that well foreknew what was to come.
The altars stand about, and eke the Nun
With sparkled tress ; the which three hundred Gods
With a loud voice doth thunder out at once,
Erebus the grisly, and Chaos huge,
And eke the threefold Goddess Hecate,
And three faces of Diana the virgin :
And sprinkles eke the water counterfeit
Like unto black Avernus' lake in hell :
And springing herbs reap'd up with brazen scythes

Were sought, after the right course of the Moon;
The venom black intermingled with milk;
The lump of flesh 'tween the new-born foals eyen
To reave, that winneth from the dam her love.
She, with the mole all in her hands devout,
Stood near the altar, bare of the one foot,
With vesture loose, the bands unlaced all;
Bent for to die, calls the Gods to record,
And guilty stars eke of her destiny:
And if there were any God that had care
Of lovers' hearts not moved with love alike,
Him she requires of justice to remember.
    It was then night; the sound and quiet sleep
Had through the earth the wearied bodies caught;
The woods, the raging seas were fallen to rest;
When that the stars had half their course declined;
The fields whist,[1] beasts, and fowls of divers hue,
And what so that in the broad lakes remained,
Or yet among the bushy thicks of brier,
Laid down to sleep by silence of the night
'Gan swage their cares, mindless of travails past.
Not so the spirit of this Phenician;
Unhappy she that on no sleep could chance,
Nor yet night's rest enter in eye or breast:
Her cares redouble; love doth rise and rage again,
And overflows with swelling storms of wrath.
Thus thinks she then, this rolls she in her mind:
    'What shall I do? shall I now bear the scorn,
For to assay mine old wooers again?
And humbly yet a Numid spouse require,
Whose marriage I have so oft disdained?
The Troyan navy, and Teucrian vile commands

    [1] Hushed, silent.

Follow shall I ? as though it should avail,
That whilom by my help they were relieved ;
Or for because with kind and mindful folk
Right well doth sit the passed thankful deed ?
Who would me suffer (admit this were my will) ?
Or me scorned to their proud ships receive ?
Oh, woe-begone ! full little knowest thou yet
The broken oaths of Laomedon's kind.
What then ? alone on merry mariners
Shall I wait ? or board them with my power
Of Tyrians assembled me about ?
And such as I with travail brought from Tyre
Drive to the seas, and force them sail again ?
But rather die, even has thou hast deserved ;
And to this woe with iron give thou end.
And thou, sister, first vanquish'd with my tears,
Thou in my rage with all these mischiefs first
Didst burden me, and yield me to my foe.
Was it not granted me from spousals free,
Like to wild beasts, to live without offence,
Without taste of such cares ? is there no faith
Reserved to the cinders of Sychee ?'
     Such great complaints brake forth out of her
          breast :
Whiles Æneas full minded to depart,
All things prepared, slept in the poop on high.
To whom in sleep the wonted Godhead's form
'Gan aye appear, returning in like shape
As seemed him ; and 'gan him thus advise :
Like unto Mercury in voice and hue,
With yellow bush, and comely limbs of youth.
' O Goddess son, in such case canst thou sleep ?
Ne yet, bestraught, the dangers dost foresee,

That compass thee? nor hear'st the fair winds
    blow?
Dido in mind rolls vengeance and deceit;
Determ'd to die, swells with unstable ire.
Wilt thou not flee whiles thou hast time of flight?
Straight shalt thou see the seas covered with sails,
The blazing brands the shore all spread with flame,
And if the morrow steal upon thee here.
Come off, have done, set all delay aside;
For full of change these women be alway.'
This said, in the dark night he 'gan him hide.
    Æneas, of this sudden vision
Adread, starts up out of his sleep in haste;
Calls up his feres: 'Awake, get up, my men,
Aboard your ships, and hoise up sail with speed;
A God me wills, sent from above again,
To haste my flight, and wreathen cables cut.
O holy God, what so thou art, we shall
Follow thee, and all blithe obey thy will;
Be at our hand, and friendly us assist;
Address the stars with prosperous influence.'
And with that word his glistering sword unsheaths;
With which drawn he the cables cut in twain.
The like desire the rest embraced all.
All thing in haste they cast, and forth they whirl;
The shores they leave; with ships the seas are
    spread;
Cutting the foam by the blue seas they sweep.
    Aurora now from Titan's purple bed
With new daylight had overspread the earth;
When by her windows the Queen the peeping day
Espied, and navy with 'splay'd sails depart
The shore, and eke the port of vessels void.

Her comely breast thrice or four times she smote
With her own hand, and tore her golden tress.
' O Jove,' quoth she, ' shall he then thus depart,
A stranger thus, and scorn our kingdom so ?
Shall not my men do on their armour prest,
And eke pursue them throughout all the town ?
Out of the road soon shall the vessel warp.
Haste on, cast flame, set sail, and wield your oars.
What said I ? but where am I ? what phrensy
Alters thy mind ?   Unhappy Dido, now
Hath thee beset a froward destiny.
Then it behoved, when thou didst give to him
His sceptre.   Lo! his faith and his right hand !
That leads with him, they say, his country Gods,
That on his back his aged father bore !
His body might I not have caught and rent ?
And in the seas drenched him and his feres ?
And from Ascanius his life with iron reft,
And set him on his father's board for meat ?
Of such debate perchance the fortune might
Have been doubtful : would God it were assay'd !
Whom should I fear, sith I myself must die ?
Might I have throwen into that navy brands,
And filled eke their decks with flaming fire,
The father, son, and all their nation
Destroy'd, and fallen myself dead over all !
Sun with thy beams, that mortal works descriest ;
And thou, Juno, that well these travails know'st ;
Proserpine, thou, upon whom folk do use
To howl, and call in forked ways by night ;
Infernal Furies eke, ye wreakers of wrong ;
And Dido's Gods, who stands at point of death,
Receive these words, and eke your heavy power

Withdraw from me, that wicked folk deserve:
And our request accept we you beseech:
If so that yonder wicked head must needs
Recover port, and sail to land of force;
And if Jove's will have so resolved it,
And such end set as no wight can foredo;
Yet at the least assailed might he be
With arms and wars of hardy nations;
From the bounds of his kingdom far exiled;
Iulus eke ravish'd out of his arms;
Driven to call for help, that he may see
The guiltless corpses of his folk lie dead:
And after hard conditions of peace,
His realm, nor life desired may he brook;
But fall before his time, ungraved amid the sands.
This I require; these words with blood I shed.
And, Tyrians, ye his stock and all his race
Pursue with hate; reward our cinders so.
No love nor league betwixt our peoples be;
And of our bones some wreaker may there spring,
With sword and flame that Troyans may pursue:
And from henceforth, when that our power may
      stretch,
Our coasts to them contrary be for aye,
I crave of God; and our streams to their floods;
Arms unto arms; and offspring of each race
With mortal war each other may fordo.'
  This said, her mind she writhed on all sides,
Seeking with speed to end her irksome life.
To Sichees' nurse, Barcen, then thus she said,
(For hers at home in ashes did remain):
'Call unto me, dear nurse, my sister Anne:
Bid her in haste in water of the flood

She sprinkle the body, and bring the beasts,
And purging sacrifice I did her shew;
So let her come: and thou thy temples bind
With sacred garlands: for the sacrifice
That I to Pluto have begun, my mind
Is to perform, and give end to these cares;
And Troyan statue throw into the flame.'
   When she had said, redouble 'gan her nurse
Her steps, forth on an aged woman's trot.
   But trembling Dido eagerly now bent
Upon her stern determination;
Her bloodshot eyes rolling within her head;
Her quivering cheeks flecked with deadly stain,
Both pale and wan to think on death to come;
Into the inward wards of her palace
She rusheth in, and clamb up, as distraught,
The burial stack, and drew the Troyan sword,
Her gift sometime, but meant to no such use.
Where when she saw his weed, and wellknowen bed,
Weeping awhile in study 'gan she stay,
Fell on the bed, and these last words she said:
   'Sweet spoils, whiles God and destinies it would,
Receive this sprite, and rid me of these cares:
I lived and ran the course fortune did grant;
And under earth my great ghost now shall wend:
A goodly town I built, and saw my walls;
Happy, alas, too happy, if these coasts
The Troyan ships had never touched aye.'
   This said, she laid her mouth close to the bed.
'Why then,' quoth she, 'unwroken shall we die?
But let us die: for this! and in this sort
It liketh us to seek the shadows dark!
And from the seas the cruel Troyan's eyes

Shall well discern this flame; and take with him
Eke these unlucky tokens of my death!'
　As she had said, her damsels might perceive
Her with these words fall pierced on a sword;
The blade embrued, and hands besprent with gore.
The clamour rang unto the palace top;
The bruit ran throughout all th' astonied town:
With wailing great, and women's shrill yelling
The roofs 'gan roar; the air resound with plaint:
As though Carthage, or th' ancient town of Tyre
With press of enter'd enemies swarmed full:
Or when the rage of furious flame doth take
The temples' tops, and mansions eke of men.
　Her sister Anne, spriteless for dread to hear
This fearful stir, with nails 'gan tear her face;
She smote her breast, and rushed through the rout:
And her dying she clepes[1] thus by her name:
　' Sister, for this with craft did you me bourd?[2]
The stack, the flame, the altars, bred they this?
What shall I first complain, forsaken wight?
Loathest thou in death thy sister's fellowship?
Thou shouldst have call'd me to like destiny;
One woe, one sword, one hour, might end us both.
This funeral stack built I with these hands,
And with this voice cleped our native Gods?
And, cruel, so absentest me from thy death?
Destroy'd thou hast, sister, both thee and me,
Thy people eke, and princes born of Tyre.
Give here; I shall with water wash her wounds;
And suck with mouth her breath, if ought be left.'
　This said, unto the high degrees she mounted,
Embracing fast her sister now half dead,

[1] Calls.　　　　　　[2] Deceive.

With wailful plaint: whom in her lap she laid,
The black swart gore wiping dry with her clothes.
But Dido striveth to lift up again
Her heavy eyen, and hath no power thereto:
Deep in her breast that fixed wound doth gape.
Thrice leaning on her elbow gan she raise
Herself upward; and thrice she overthrew
Upon the bed: ranging with wand'ring eyes
The skies for light, and wept when she it found.
    Almighty Juno having ruth by this
Of her long pains, and eke her lingering death,
From heaven she sent the Goddess Iris down,
The throwing sprite, and jointed limbs to loose.
For that neither by lot of destiny,
Nor yet by kindly death she perished,
But wretchedly before her fatal day,
And kindled with a sudden rage of flame,
Proserpine had not from her head bereft
The golden hair, nor judged her to hell.
The dewy Iris thus with golden wings,
A thousand hues shewing against the Sun,
Amid the skies then did she fly adown
On Dido's head: where as she 'gan alight,
'This hair,' quod she, 'to Pluto consecrate,
Commanded I reave; and thy spirit unloose
From this body.'   And when she thus had sai
With her right hand she cut the hair in twain:
And therewithal the kindly heat 'gan quench,
And into wind the life forthwith resolve.

The two following poems are given from a very curious MS. of the time of Henry the VIIIth, belonging to the Duke of Devonshire. The greater part of the poems in that MS. have the names, or the initials of their respective authors subscribed. The signatures originally affixed to those here printed have been much effaced. What remains of them, however, is sufficient to lead to some conjecture. The first is subscribed "Finis q^d. W   t;" the second, "Finis q^d. S   e." Respecting the first of these names I apprehend no doubt can be entertained, especially as a large number of the poems in the volume bear Wyatt's signature. That the latter name was designed for Surrey's, I think extremely probable; for his name was then generally spelt "Surreye:" and the letter preceding the final "e," though erased in part, seems to have been "y." I believe that many compositions have been ascribed to authors on presumptive evidence less strong than the present. It should be observed, that Surrey and Wyatt were in the habit of frequently communicating their verses to each other. See the poems in this volume, which begin; "As oft as I behold and see;" p. 37: and "Love that liveth and reigneth in my thought;" p. 12.—*Dr. Nott.*

PRIMUS.

MY fearful hope from me is fled,
  Which of long time hath been my guide.
  Now faithful trust is in his stead,
  And bids me set all fear aside.
O' ruth it is, I not deny,

All lovers may not live in ease.
Yet some by hap doth hit truly;
So like may I, if that she please.

Why! so it is a gift, ye wot,
By nature one to love another.
And since that love doth fall by lot;
Then why not I, as well as other.

It may so be the cause is why,
She knoweth no part to my poor mind:
But yet as one assuredly
I speak nothing but as I find.

If Nature will, it shall so be:
No reason ruleth Fantasy.
Yet in this case, as seemeth me,   ·
I take all thing indifferently.

Yet uncertain I will rejoice,
And think to have, though yet thou hast.
I put my chance unto her choice
With patience, for power is past.

No! no! I know the like is fair
Without disdain or cruelty:
And so to end, from all despair;
Until I find the contrary.

SECUNDUS.

OUR fearful hope cannot prevail;
Nor yet faithful trust also.
Some thinks to hit, ofttimes do fail;
Whereby they change their wealth to
    woe.
What though! in that yet put no trust:
But always after as ye see.
For say your will, and do your lust;
There is no place for you to be.
   No such within; ye are far out.
Your labour lost ye hope to save.
But once I put ye out of doubt;
The thing is had that ye would have.
   Though to remain without remorse,
And pitiless to be opprest;
Yet is the course of Love, by force
To take all things unto the best.
   Well! yet beware, if thou be wise:
And leave thy hope thy heat to cool:
For fear lest she thy love despise,
Reputing thee but as a fool.
   Since this to follow of force thou must,
And by no reason can refrain;
Thy chance shall change thy least mistrust;
As thou shalt prove unto thy pain.

When with such pain thou shalt be paid,
The which shall pass all remedy ;
Then think on this that I have said ;
And blame thy foolish Fantasy.

FINIS.

CHISWICK PRESS :—C. WHITTINGHAM AND CO., TOOKS COURT,
CHANCERY LANE.

CPSIA information can be obtained
at www.ICGtesting.com
Printed in the USA
LVHW081207020720
659542LV00011B/1344